Praise for *Fortune in Your Hands*

"Alaric Albertsson brings Witches back to the magickal art of playing cards, an often forgotten part of our Craft. As he takes us through the history and clears up misconceptions, shares the esoteric theories of the elements and numbers, and, most importantly, teaches the practical applications, we can learn from him as a trusted magickal elder passing on an important part of the modern Witch's legacy to us."

—**CHRISTOPHER PENCZAK,** author of the Temple of Witchcraft series

FORTUNE IN YOUR HANDS

About the Author

Alaric Albertsson (Iowa) is the author of several books on magic and spirituality, including *A Handbook of Saxon Sorcery and Magic* and *To Walk a Pagan Path*. He has served as vice president and was on the board of directors of the Heartland Spiritual Alliance, and has served as the Anglo-Saxon Vice Chieftain for Ár nDraíocht Féin's Germanic kin, Eldr ok Iss.

Albertsson first embraced polytheism in the summer of 1971. At that time he was introduced to the folk tradition of spellcasting and divination with playing cards. Over the past five decades, Albertsson's personal spiritual practice has developed as a synthesis of Anglo-Saxon tradition, folk magic, herbal studies, and rune lore. Visit him on Facebook.

FORTUNE IN YOUR HANDS

A Witch's Guide to Playing Card Divination and Magic

ALARIC ALBERTSSON

Llewellyn Publications • Woodbury, Minnesota

FIRST EDITION
First Printing, 2024

Book design by Donna Burch-Brown
Cover design by Kevin R. Brown

Llewellyn Publications is a registered trademark of Llewellyn
    Worldwide Ltd.

Library of Congress Cataloging-in-Publication Data
Names: Albertsson, Alaric, author.
Title: Fortune in your hands : a witch's guide to playing card divination
    and magic / by Alaric Albertsson.
Description: First edition. | Woodbury, Minnesota : Llewellyn
    Worldwide, 2024. | Summary: "This is a book about divination using
    ordinary playing cards. Card interpretations are broken down by
    their numerological significance and the elemental correspondences
    of the four suits. Includes a discussion of options for laying out the
    cards, the ethics of divination, and a chapter exploring the use of
    playing cards for spellcasting"— Provided by publisher.
Identifiers: LCCN 2024009011 (print) | LCCN 2024009012 (ebook)
    cards, the ethics of divination, and a chapter exploring the use of
    | ISBN 9780738777894 (paperback) | ISBN 9780738777993 (ebook)
Subjects: LCSH: Fortune-telling by cards. | Playing cards. | Divination.
    cards, the ethics of divination, and a chapter exploring the use of
    | Witchcraft.
Classification: LCC BF1878 .A436 2024 (print) | LCC BF1878 (ebook)
    | DDC 133.3/242—dc23/eng/20240412
LC record available at https://lccn.loc.gov/2024009011
LC ebook record available at https://lccn.loc.gov/2024009012

Llewellyn Publications
A Division of Llewellyn Worldwide Ltd.
2143 Wooddale Drive
Woodbury, MN 55125-2989
www.llewellyn.com

Printed in the United States of America

Other Books by Alaric Albertsson

A Handbook of Saxon Sorcery & Magic
(Llewellyn, 2017)

To Walk a Pagan Path
(Llewellyn, 2013)

Contents

Introduction

Sortilege, the casting or drawing of lots, is the most common form of divination. The first method that I learned in 1971 made use of ordinary playing cards. None of the witches I knew then were familiar with Tarot. In any event, Tarot decks were extremely rare and difficult to come by until U.S. Games began marketing the Rider-Waite deck, which they had only just started to do. And there were no New Age stores to visit. Like the medieval witches did with their cauldrons and broomsticks, we made do with everyday items around the house.

This does not mean we were entirely without resources. In libraries and bookstores we found inspiration through the writings of authors like Paul Huson, Louise Huebner, and Sybil Leek. Huebner in particular advocated the use of playing cards as a magical tool. In fact, the twelve-card layout presented in this book is an adaptation of a layout she presented in *Power Through Witchcraft* (Nash Publishing, 1961). Our witchcraft back then consisted entirely of ordinary things: playing cards, candles, perhaps a handful of salt. It would be several more years before my first formal initiation, which would then be followed by several others. However, the one I take the most pride in was my dedication as a Seax *gesith* in 1975. It was a new tradition, with no claims of antiquity, and it set me on a path of Saxon spirituality that I still follow to this day. This, in turn, led to a study of the Old English runes, a set of symbols used for magic, divination, and writing. I found a great deal of value in runic divination. Nevertheless, even now I will still pick up a deck of playing cards if I want insight into some situation.

Why? Because at this moment playing cards still work better for me.

Every symbol set is a sort of language and, like every language, each has its own finite, limited vocabulary. In most forms of sortilege, the words—the symbols—have very broad meanings, but there are nevertheless some concepts that are more easily expressed than others. This is why many Tarot readers favor one or two specific decks. The images printed on those decks communicate more readily with them. If I have any kind of question regarding spirituality or personal growth, the runes are my choice for seeking an answer. But very often, for more mundane questions I am likely to turn to playing cards.

And yes, I also have a deck of Tarot cards. I am just not very good with Tarot cards. Over the years I have found that my psychic faculty responds better to more abstract symbols than to specific images.

Another thing that emerged over the years was my awareness of a pattern in the interpretation of playing cards. When this method of divination was presented to me, I had to memorize the meaning of each card by rote, and the meanings varied from one source to another. But beneath it all, I began to detect patterns, and as my understanding of magic expanded, I was able to identify those patterns. The cards reflect a blend of Western elemental theory and basic numerology. Understanding these patterns is much easier than memorizing the individual meanings of fifty-two different cards.

Within the pages of this book, I share my understanding of playing card divination with you. It will still take some effort and practice on your part, but I think you will find that the cards are relatively easy to interpret when you understand the elemental and numerological patterns. A good seer should master several methods of perceiving the forces that shape our destiny, and playing card divination is a method that has proven itself over time. Indeed, it was the only method I used for several years, and it has served me very well.

I would like to thank everyone who has made this book possible. Special thanks to my acquisitions editor, Elysia Gallo, and to my production editor, Andrea Neff. Thanks also to the cover artist (the talented Kevin Brown), to the production designer (Donna Burch-Brown), and to everyone else who does not get their name on the front of the book, even though their work is so important to its construction.

It is my sincere hope that *Fortune in Your Hands* will lead you, the reader, to a wonderful path of divination and magic. Take up your cards, trust in your intuition, and always keep that magic alive.

~Alaric Albertsson

One
Why Playing Cards?

When I first learned a method of divination, it was with a deck of playing cards. Yes, I mean everyday, ordinary playing cards. I had been using playing cards in this way for a couple of years before I even heard of Tarot cards, and then another year or so passed by before I discovered runes. I do enjoy working with runes and exploring their mysteries. For me, the runes are sacred symbols. Divination is only one of the ways that I interact with them. And like most contemporary Pagans, I'm also acquainted with the Tarot and its symbolism. There are other symbol sets used for divination, often based on ancient alphabets, as well as a seemingly infinite variety of oracle decks, but I frequently just pick up a deck of playing cards when I have a question to resolve or I want to work a spell that can be best expressed through the symbolism found in Hearts, Clubs, Diamonds, and Spades.

There are some people who believe playing cards to be a modern contrivance with no real substance or tradition behind them, but this is simply not true. In fact, playing cards may be among the most traditional magical tools available to us today.

Why? Because for most people throughout history, it was the commonplace things, items that were readily available, that were used for magic and divination. European peasants had no access to ritual swords, Tarot cards, or exotic herbs, but they did have knives, yarrow plants, and pools of water, so those were the tools they used to look for future influences. They used commonplace things, and what is more commonplace than a deck of cards? Even before mass production, these were more readily available to most people than a Tarot deck would have been. Today, decks are sold everywhere: supermarkets, gas stations, discount stores. You probably have one or more decks of playing cards sitting around somewhere in your home right now.

Modern witches will often eschew decks of playing cards because they are not perceived to be an old tradition, but these same people do not hesitate to use computers, automobiles, and phones to connect with each other and enhance their magical practice. Witches (and other magical people) use many tools today that are commonplace even if they are not exactly ancient. When I brew a potion, I use my electric range, even though my ancestors relied on cauldrons over open fires to infuse their herbs. And I usually drive alone or with a friend to the Midsummer ritual rather take a horse or ride in a wagon. So when I want a reading or need to cast a spell, I am as likely to use a deck of playing cards as I would any other tool. I make use of the tools and devices that I have available.

And just because playing cards are commonplace does not mean they are not traditional. Playing cards have a history as long and prestigious as that of the Tarot deck.

A Brief History of Playing Cards

Cards were introduced into Europe in the 1300s. They probably came through the Mamluk Sultanate, a government that ruled Egypt and part of western Arabia from the 1200s to the 1500s. However, by then cards had already been around for centuries in other parts of the world. The first playing cards were printed in China during the Tang Dynasty. These earliest Chinese decks were created during the 800s using woodblock printing. They did not have suits or numbers, but by the time playing cards migrated west through Persia and Egypt and then into Europe, they had evolved into decks with four suits similar to those we are familiar with today in our modern decks of cards. The Egyptian deck had twelve pip cards and three court cards, much like a contemporary card deck; however, the court cards featured abstract designs rather than images of people. This may have been due to Islamic prohibitions against depicting sentient beings.

The first European decks had suits of Coins, Cups, Polo-Sticks, and Swords. The Polo-Sticks soon became Clubs or Cudgels, since polo was not a widespread sport in Europe at that time. The symbols of these four suits continued to evolve with different regional images, and playing cards today have various forms that can be grouped into general categories of French, Latin, and Germanic. The playing cards used today in both the United Kingdom and the United States are in the French category, and those are the decks I am referencing throughout this book when I say "playing cards."

Cards in the Latin category are used in Italy and Spain. These also have four suits, but instead of the symbols of Diamonds, Hearts, Clubs, and Spades, they have imagery closer to that of the earliest European decks: Coins, Cups, Clubs (or Batons), and Swords. In northern Italian cities in the mid-1400s, Latin decks of cards were designed with an additional "trump" suit consisting of twenty-two cards. These altered decks were called *carte da trionfi*, or triumph cards, although today we know them as Tarot. The oldest surviving decks of Tarot cards were painted for the Visconti-Sforza family, who ruled the city of Milan at the time. Like our modern decks, these were used for playing card games.

Decks of triumph cards were expensive and rare, but they continued to be used for both games and gambling by those who could afford them. The trump cards in particular had complex images. Each was a work of art expressing Roman Catholic symbolism on cards with titles like the Pope, the Devil, Judgment Day, and so on. Associating the trump cards with the Church was probably a good idea, for card games were often condemned by both religious and secular authorities back then, so much so that cards were sometimes referred to as "the devil's picture book."

Despite this condemnation, card games remained a popular pastime. We can assume that both playing cards and Tarot cards were also used for divination occasionally. This practice is called *cartomancy*, which is just a fancy way of saying card divination. There are literally countless "-mancies," using everything from fire (pyromancy) to ghosts (necromancy) to the behavior of cats (ailuromancy). Cartomancy falls into a more finite category of divination known as *sortilege*, or the drawing of lots. This includes divination with dice or with runes as well as divination with cards. The practice of sortilege requires a specific set of symbols that are drawn at random and then interpreted.

Sortilege can be practiced with any closed set of symbols (and divination with playing cards can be dated to at least 1540), but the Tarot deck started to take on a more overt mystical significance in the eighteenth century. A Protestant minister in France by the name of Antoine Court speculated that the Tarot was somehow derived from the Egyptian *Book of Thoth*. He also connected the cards of the trump suit with the twenty-two letters of the Hebrew alphabet. Court's essays fostered more interest in the Tarot, but there was still no real advantage to divination with a deck that was more expensive and difficult to come by. Although the trump suit had complex illustrations, the other four suits differed little from other Latin decks of playing cards that were being used throughout Italy. An Eight of Swords, for example, was simply a picture of eight swords, with no further illustration to convey any meaning for interpretation.

This changed in the early twentieth century thanks to two occultists, Arthur Edward Waite and Pamela Colman Smith. Both were members of the Hermetic Order of the Golden Dawn, and both moved on to the Rectified Rite of the Golden Dawn when the former organization split up. Smith was an accomplished artist, and in 1909, Waite commissioned her to design images for all 78 cards of the Tarot deck. A year later, the new deck was published by William Rider & Son of London. With illustrations on all of the cards suggesting interpretations, it was significantly different from earlier decks. The Rider-Waite deck had less overt Christian imagery, changing the Pope card to the Hierophant and the Papess to the High Priestess, and it conveyed more mystic symbolism that reflected a Golden Dawn influence. More importantly, however, all of the suits, not just the trump suit, were illustrated with Smith's descriptive images showing their meanings as she and Waite interpreted them.

These images gave the new Rider-Waite deck (now often called Waite-Smith or Rider-Waite-Smith) an advantage over playing cards and the earlier Tarot decks. If a reader could not remember the meaning of the Ten of Swords, for example, the image of a person sprawled on the ground and impaled with swords clearly suggested something bad. Like the cards of the trump suit, every card in the Rider-Waite deck had an image illustrating its general meaning.

Tarot decks were still far more expensive than decks of playing cards and were often difficult to find at all. Over the years, Tarot became more popular, though, and today it is the most common method employed in divination.

So why bother with playing cards at all? Sure, they are less expensive than Tarot cards, but most Tarot decks today are now priced affordably. There are several other reasons to use playing cards for divination and magic, however.

First, the use of playing cards is exotic. That does not mean it is necessarily better, but you will have a skill that is not often seen in our magical communities these days. The overwhelming majority of people who read cards now use either a Tarot deck or an oracle deck. If you want to stand apart from the crowd, consider divination with playing cards.

Second, the very fact that playing cards have no specific imagery can allow the psychic faculty to come into play more readily, although this will vary from reader to reader. Because of the lack of imagery, playing cards have more in common with divinatory practices such as pyromancy (fire gazing) and crystallomancy (crystal gazing) than with most modern Tarot decks. The meanings derived from such practices are more open-ended; what a fire gazer sees in the flames is not defined by an image on a card. Likewise, an interpretation of the Ten of Spades can be more intuitive and nuanced than one based on the horrific Waite-Smith image of a man impaled by ten swords. For some people, the images on a modern Tarot deck are extremely helpful, but for others, those same images can restrict the flow of intuitive impressions.

Because of this lack of imagery, the meanings attributed to playing cards will often vary from one reader to another. You may discover that the Three of Hearts holds a special meaning for you that is not mentioned in this book. This could also occur for a Tarot reader, finding something personal and unique in the Three of Cups, but it is less likely because there is a specific image on the card. In addition to the three cups on this Tarot card, there are usually three young women, often (but not always) dancing. Essentially, an artist designing a Tarot deck is telling you how to interpret each card. By contrast, divination with playing cards can be a very personal experience precisely because they lack these illustrations. The meaning you associate with a particular card can even change over time as your own personality and destiny grow and shift into new directions.

Finally, like other symbol sets used for sortilege, playing cards speak their own language. If you have already mastered more than one method of divination, you will understand what I mean by this. Runic symbols give a different sort of reading than do ogham symbols, and both of these are a little different from the readings you will get from Tarot cards. I have found that playing cards tend to address events and individuals around me, whereas both runes and Tarot are more likely to address personal, internal changes. Your experience may vary, of course, but you will almost surely find that your readings with playing cards have a flavor of their own.

A Pattern in the Cards

Perhaps the most daunting aspect of using playing cards for divination is learning the meaning of each card without having illustrations to serve as reminders. This is also true of other sets of symbols such as runes and oghams, as well as the earlier, pre-Smith Tarot decks. The meanings of runes can be easier to learn than those of a deck of playing cards simply because there are not nearly as many symbols to memorize. Depending on which runes you wish to study, there will be between sixteen and thirty-three symbols to master. (The set of runes most often sold in New Age stores, the Elder Futhark, has twenty-four symbols.) Celtic Pagans who use the oghams for divination have twenty-five symbols to learn. Compared to these other symbol sets, learning the fifty-two meanings in a deck of playing cards can seem like quite a hurdle.

When I learned to read cards, I had to memorize the meanings and connotations of each card by rote, which was really difficult. Over time, however, I began to notice certain patterns that would have made the task much easier. As I learned more about Pagan philosophy and occult sciences, I saw a relationship between the card interpretations and both numerology and elemental theory. These were *general* patterns, guidelines, with exceptions that undoubtedly arose from personal experiences. The person who taught me how to read cards surely included some of her own interpretations, and over the years I have undoubtedly added some of my own. This is inevitable with a set of symbols that aren't clearly illustrated, as they are in modern Tarot decks, nor accompanied by historical lore, like the various Germanic runes. Again, whether this is a hindrance or a benefit depends on your approach to divination and magic.

An approach to card reading based on elemental theory and numerology means you need to learn the connotations of only thirteen symbols (four elements and nine numbers). You can then combine the stability of the number four with the emotional association of the Water element and readily perceive the Four of Hearts as a representation of an emotionally stable relationship. It represents friendship. This pattern will help you understand the meanings of all of the cards from the aces to the tens. It doesn't apply to the court cards, but those cards *do* have imagery that will help you remember their meanings, and the elemental influence applies to them as well as to the numbered cards.

I have included an appendix in the back of the book with keywords to help you get a feeling for these elemental and numerological concepts. It will help to refer to it frequently as you develop a relationship with the cards.

Of course, there is more to reading cards than looking at the Four of Hearts and seeing *stability + emotion*. In a sense, the cards themselves don't "mean" anything at all; they are just playing cards. The interpretation, the meaning, comes from within the reader, who uses the cards to stimulate their psychic faculty. Throughout this book, we will be discussing the meanings of the cards, but this basic truth must be kept in mind as you master the art of reading playing cards. Although the cards have distinct implications, the meaning of any given card is mutable and will vary depending on the immediate situation. It will depend on who you are reading for and on what you, the reader, bring to the table yourself. The aforementioned Four of Hearts may come to have some personal meaning to you other than what we discuss in this book. You may even find that one or more of the cards, for you, indicate specific people. For the person who taught me how to read playing cards, the Jack of Diamonds represented her partner, although the card did not have this meaning when she was reading for somebody else. It certainly didn't represent her partner when she was giving a reading for me, because I didn't even know the guy!

When I read playing cards myself, I look at the entire layout before focusing on any one card. The surrounding cards can not only influence the meaning of a card but can actually change it entirely. I have found that in a layout where the surrounding cards indicate a chaotic situation, the Four of Hearts (*stability* + *emotion*) is probably advising the querent to remain calm until the circumstances change. The stability of this card is negated by the cards around it. In this situation, the card is asking for stability rather than announcing its presence. And I am not picking on the Four of Hearts; this mutable quality is true of all of the cards.

Preparing Your Deck

So how do you begin working with playing cards as a tool for divination? First, obviously, you need a deck of cards. If you feel more comfortable doing so, you can purchase a new deck specifically for divination, but this is not really necessary. A deck that you have in a drawer or on a shelf somewhere in your home can work just as well, and from a metaphysical perspective, it may be an even better choice because it is already a part of your life.

Some people want to use a new deck because they are afraid that an older deck may have picked up some bad energy, but those influences can be readily cleared away, as we will discuss shortly.

If you have more than one deck to choose from, examine your choices closely before deciding which will be your deck for divination and magic. Playing cards are such an ordinary part of our world that we tend to take them for granted and assume that all decks are the same, but they are not. Different decks have distinct, if subtle, differences in style, especially in the court cards (the King, Queen, and Jack of each suit). The King of Hearts in the Hoyle deck is holding his sword at a different angle than is the King in a deck of Tuxedo cards. They also have different crowns and different designs on their royal garments. These distinctions may not seem significant, but I think it is important to use a deck that resonates with you. The backs of the cards will also have a design that may inspire your intuition as you shuffle the deck. No one deck of playing cards is inherently better than any other, and any deck can work for you, but if you have a choice, then look closely at the cards before deciding which deck you want to use.

Whichever deck you choose and wherever it comes from, there is one thing you need to do to prepare it before you begin using it for divination: remove the Jokers.

There is a persistent claim that the Joker is a remnant of the Tarot's trump suit, specifically that it is a carry-over of the card known as the Fool. This idea comes from the mistaken belief that playing cards evolved from the Tarot. The truth is that the Joker card was invented in the United States during the 1860s for the game of Euchre. Originally that extra card was called the "Best Bower," but within a few years the card began to take on the name of Joker, which may have come from the German spelling of Euchre (*Juker*). Like the Fool card of the Tarot, the Jokers were created to be trump cards, but otherwise the two are unrelated.

Of course, there are no hard-and-fast rules about reading cards, and that includes the rule I just gave you about removing the Jokers. I learned to read cards without using the Jokers, but Tarot cards, as well as our normal card decks, were originally created for playing games, so assigning some meaning to the Jokers and including them in your readings does have considerable historical precedent. After all, this is how all cards became tools for divination. I have heard that some people interpret the black Joker with the meaning attributed to the Fool card of the Tarot, and the red Joker with the meaning attributed to the Magician. In my personal experience, I have never felt any need to add these cards to the already complex and well-balanced set of symbols found in the four suits in a deck of cards, but I am not going to tell you that it's "wrong" to do so.

After you remove the Jokers (assuming you do this), there are two other things you might want to do to prepare your deck for divination and magic. Just like removing the Jokers, both of these are optional. First, you may want to cleanse the deck. This is more likely to be a concern with an older deck, especially if you feel that your readings will be influenced by countless games of Canasta or Bridge, but even a newly purchased deck was manufactured, packaged, and sold by people who had specific intentions, desires, and feelings as they created it and put it on a store shelf.

To cleanse a deck, place it in a small bowl or similar container and cover it completely with salt. Cleansing and protection are the magical properties of salt. Be sure to bury the deck completely under the salt. As you do this, you may wish to say a few words that are appropriate to your personal spiritual path or just say something like this: "Salt is the crystal of purification. Let it drive out any spirit that dwells within, about, or around these cards." Then leave the cards buried in the salt overnight.

You can keep the cards in their box when you bury the deck, but the process is more effective without the box, leaving the cards in direct contact with the salt. A few grains may work their way between the cards, but this will not be a problem. Any stray bits of salt will fall out later when you shuffle the deck a few times.

Whether or not you cleanse the deck, you may wish to consecrate it to its future purpose as a tool for divination or magic. Depending on your inclination and your spiritual path, this can be accomplished with anything from a short, simple prayer to a complex ritual. For Saxon Pagans, I would suggest a prayer asking for Woden's guidance, while Hellenic or Roman Pagans might solicit the same from Apollo. Wiccans will probably prefer to consecrate their decks within a magic circle. I cannot tell you how to consecrate your deck, because it depends entirely on your own spiritual orientation; however, I do think it is important to assign purpose to your deck through a prayer or ritual of some kind before you begin to use it. By doing this, you affirm that your work with the cards is more than just a game. To further affirm this, your deck should never be used for card games after you have consecrated it to a greater purpose.

You can control your own actions, but the day may come when somebody else picks up your cards and uses them for a couple of hands of Old Maid. This could happen. After all, your deck does look like any other deck of playing cards. If this happens, it doesn't mean you have to burn the deck and start over with a new one. Just cleanse the deck with salt and consecrate it again to its greater purpose, and everything will be fine. And do not blame your friend—it was just as much your fault for leaving your deck lying around.

This brings up the question of where to keep your deck once it has been consecrated and you have started working with it. You have two options. Neither is necessarily better, but you should pick one and stick with it.

The first option is to treat your deck as something sacred and set apart from the mundane world. Some people find this gives their decks more power and significance. Your deck should be wrapped in either linen or silk when not in use, and should be touched only when you are working with it. Some readers who use this approach never let anyone else, even querents (the people they are reading for), touch their decks for any reason. The deck is never touched or seen except when employed for divination or magic.

The second option is almost the direct opposite, where a bond is formed between the reader and the deck through direct proximity. This option makes use of the fundamental magical law of contagion, which states that any two things in contact have a link to each other. Although you will not be playing card games with your deck, it should be kept close to you as much as possible. If you keep it handy, you may find yourself engaged in impromptu readings more often, pulling out and considering one or more cards simply because it is convenient to do so. For the record, this is the option I prefer. My own deck is sitting right here to the left of my keyboard as I write this. Having my cards close to me creates a connection to them, and for me this is more empowering than keeping them wrapped in linen and set apart from the world.

Once you have your deck prepared and ready, the next step is to understand the general connotations of each card. Let's begin by looking at the four suits and how their meanings are related to the four elements.

The Suits and the Elements

An *element* is a fundamental component. In this chapter and throughout this book, any use of this word refers to the five elements of traditional Western European philosophy, not to the atomic elements as defined by modern chemistry. Other than a shared name, the two concepts are entirely unrelated.

An understanding of elemental theory will help you interpret cards. The four suits correspond to the four base elements: Diamonds with Earth, Hearts with Water, Clubs with Fire, and Spades with Air. These elements are terms describing states of energy, and familiarizing yourself with each of them can give you insights into what the cards are conveying. An abundance of Clubs, for example, suggests transformation and change coming into your life (or into the life of the person you are reading for).

A Brief History of Western Elements

Elemental theory evolved in locations as diverse as India, Europe, and China through observation of the natural world. Although the terminology differs from one culture to the next, the basic ideas are similar in these philosophies. A study of Ayurvedic elements and Chinese elements can be fascinating in itself, but our focus in this book will be on European elemental theory and its influence on the Western worldview.

As a science, elemental theory advanced as generations of philosopher-scientists compared their own observations with earlier ideas. There were debates about how many elements existed and about which of those, if any, was a primordial element that the others were derived from. Thales (c. 624–c. 546 BCE) argued that Water was the first element from which everything else originated. Heraclitus (c. 535–c. 475 BCE) later claimed Fire to be the primordial substance. As with any science, these ideas were tested and debated, and altered when necessary, in an endless quest for a greater understanding of the universe.

By the middle of the fifth century BCE, there was a general acceptance of the existence of four elements designated as Earth, Water, Air, and Fire. It was at this time that the Greek physician Hippocrates of Kos developed his theory of *humours*. The humours were essentially the four elements with respect to the human body. Hippocrates defined these as black bile (Earth), phlegm (Water), blood (Air), and yellow bile (Fire). Good health could be achieved, according to Hippocrates, by maintaining a balance of these humours. This idea of balancing the elements can also be found in both Ayurveda and Traditional Chinese Medicine. In Europe, the theory of humours was so successful that it remained a fundamental system for centuries. Hippocrates eventually came to be known as the "father of medicine."

These four elements—Earth, Water, Air, and Fire—were not perceived as static substances but rather as states of existence related to temperature and humidity. Earth is cold and dry, Water is cold and moist, Air is warm and moist, and Fire is warm and dry. Aristotle described how the elements transform into each other with changes in either temperature or humidity. These concepts shaped European thought, which is why even today English speakers are likely to say that they have "caught a cold" to describe a physical illness brought on by what early Europeans would have described as an excess of either phlegm (Water) or black bile (Earth).

Eventually a fifth element of *Aether* was acknowledged, bringing elemental theory in Europe more in line with those in India and China. By that time, however, the four element model of Earth, Water, Air, and Fire was already well established and continued to shape Western perception. Everything in existence—every food, herb, cardinal direction, and season of the year—was associated with an element. With the pervasive influence of the elements, it should come as no surprise that the suits in every deck of playing cards are assigned to the four elements.

Incidentally, these same four elemental associations also hold true for the suits of Coins, Cups, Swords, and Batons found in a Tarot deck, but here we will examine the elements as they relate to playing cards. In the back of this book is an appendix with keywords to help you gain a mastery of these elemental influences.

Diamonds (Earth)

The suit of Diamonds reflects the element of Earth. The keyword to remember for this suit is *fortune*. The gemstones and precious metals that we identify with fortune are physical manifestations of this cool, dry element.

When a Diamond card appears in a reading, it usually indicates something material and substantial. Very often it has to do with wealth, but this could be somebody else's wealth or it could be a loss of wealth. What a Diamond card has to say about wealth depends on which card it is and which other cards fall around it. Diamonds can also represent your reputation or social standing, as these can influence and be influenced by wealth.

Unless you were born into wealth or are lucky enough to win the lottery, money doesn't just suddenly appear, so the Diamond suit often refers to one's career or business interests. One of the Diamond cards might indicate something about your work conditions. The Diamonds can also describe the general economy, since that affects your wealth along with everyone else's. These cards can represent your stocks or investments, if you have any.

But fortune, whether good or ill, comes in forms other than wealth, and this is also reflected in the suit of Diamonds. This suit can indicate any kind of success or achievement. Diamonds might point to recognition of your efforts or to finally attaining a goal. And as I have said, Diamonds might address your reputation. Anything like this affects your personal fortune, which encompasses much more than just monetary wealth.

As cards of fortune, Diamonds often indicate sheer luck. Of course, both personal success and the acquisition of wealth often involve some degree of luck. Diamonds can speak to you of your destiny.

Competition and the drive for success and wealth can bring out the worst in people, and this is seen in the court cards of the suit of Diamonds. Court cards, as we will discuss in the next chapter, represent people. In the suit of Diamonds, the people indicated by the court cards are not completely trustworthy. They aren't necessarily bad people, but they have their own agendas, which might not be beneficial to you. Depending on where the Diamond court card appears in a reading, it could also indicate an ambitious person who could be a valuable ally.

I have heard that the Diamond court cards indicate blond people; however, this has not been my experience. It seems to me that the likelihood of meeting a blond has more to do with where you live and the social circles you travel in rather than the cards drawn in a divination. Nevertheless, the claim has been made often enough that I feel I should mention it here. In the first chapter, I talked about how playing cards can take on special, personal meanings. If you notice that the Diamond court cards are speaking to you of blond people, then accept that as your personal truth.

Hearts (Water)

The suit of Hearts reflects the element of Water. The keyword to remember for this suit is *emotion*. In astrology, the Water signs are the most emotional signs of the zodiac, and water often symbolizes emotions in dream interpretation.

The Hearts speak to the part of you that the early Anglo-Saxons called the *myne*, which includes both your emotions and your memories. The more we love (or hate) something, the more that person or thing becomes embedded in our memory. This can be good or bad, depending on whether we want to remember a particular person, situation, or event. On one hand we want to remember and be remembered by our loved ones, but those same memories are the cause of ongoing grief when we lose someone we love or when we suffer an unpleasant experience.

When Hearts appear in a divination, they almost always address your emotional relationships. When looking at a card in this suit, it is tempting to see romance in the valentine appearance of its symbol, but the Hearts are just as likely to indicate platonic or familial relationships. Romantic love is only one small part of the emotional spectrum. The relationships indicated by Heart cards can also vary greatly from one individual to another. For a married woman in her thirties or forties, Hearts could indicate friendships that mean a lot to her rather than an unexpected and perhaps undesirable romantic entanglement. For an elderly widower, the same cards could point to his children and grandchildren.

For some people, the Hearts do indicate romance. Again, depending on the individual, a Heart card can indicate a storybook romance leading to a long-term relationship, but it can just as easily infer a passionate, lustful sexual encounter that will end before sunrise. Interpreting the Heart cards is simple when reading for yourself, but you must rely entirely on your psychic talent when reading for someone else unless you know that person very well.

Emotional relationships do not evolve in a vacuum. Sometimes the Hearts can indicate social situations rather than individual connections. These can range from large parties to more sedate pastimes or hobbies, as long as the latter are not solitary activities. Hearts often speak of social events. The Hearts might indicate evenings playing games with friends around the dining room table, but not a long night playing video games alone.

The court cards of the Hearts suit are almost the antithesis of the Diamond court cards. Whereas the latter suggest people to be wary of, the Heart court cards are usually people you can be comfortable with. It is very likely that you already know these people. If the court card of this suit indicates a stranger, it will be a person who is easy to connect with. Heart court cards are often passionate, emotional people.

Spades (Air)

The suit of Spades reflects the element of Air. The keyword to remember for this suit is *movement*. Think of a breeze moving through your hair and across your skin.

One thing you will notice in your readings is that the "cold" suits of Diamonds and Hearts (Earth and Water) tend to indicate a degree of stability, whereas the "warm" suits of Spades and Clubs (Air and Fire) speak of change. Movement is change, sometimes pleasant, often disruptive and undesirable. If you can maintain control, movement can push you toward your goals. If not, it can blow you off course.

Wherever Spades appear in a reading, you can expect disruption. Often this disruption can be overcome and you can achieve your goals, but it may require more work than expected and the rewards may be less than expected. Spades often mess with your plans.

In fact, they will *usually* mess with your plans if you do not meet the challenges they present head-on.

To understand the suit of Spades, imagine being buffeted by a wind. Even a slight breeze will blow away papers and cards. A stronger wind lifts, moves, or pushes over heavier objects, and a powerful gale can destroy almost everything in its path. But with effort and planning, it is possible to harness the wind to move ships across the sea or to grind hard grain into flour. The Spades are that buffeting wind. They do not always predict failure, but they indicate chaos and challenges that can often *lead* to failure.

The Spade court cards, as you might expect, are people who will try to bring this sort of disruption into your life. Whereas the Diamond court cards are people with agendas that might just happen to conflict with your goals, the Spades are more likely to be people who are targeting you personally. The King of Diamonds could be one of your friends, but the King of Spades certainly is not! The antagonism may be due to something that has occurred between you and the other person, but it is a rift that will be difficult, if not impossible, to mend. Or the other person may just dislike you on some irrational, visceral level. Whatever the source of the other person's hostility, and whether or not there is any justification for it, a court card from the suit of Spades is a warning to watch out for that person.

Clubs (Fire)

The suit of Clubs reflects the element of Fire. The keyword to remember for this suit is *transformation*. Fire always transforms what it touches. It transforms wood into ash, water into steam. Blacksmiths use fire to transform iron into blades and tools.

Fire is often a destructive force. A forest fire may clear the way for new growth, but that is little consolation for the woodland denizens caught up in the conflagration. The transformation indicated by Clubs is often painful, even when the end result is something more than residual ashes.

There is a similarity between the Clubs and Spades in that both point toward chaos. However, with Spades this is an external force often beyond your direct control, whereas when Clubs appear in a reading, you usually are the cause of the problem or you have a significant influence over it. In this respect, Clubs are rather nice because they indicate that you are in control of the situation even if this is not readily apparent to you. It is your actions and choices that will affect the final outcome.

A simple lack of awareness is very often the cause of a situation described by a card from the suit of Clubs. Very often, becoming conscious of the problem and changing your attitude and choices is enough to remedy the situation. Not everyone is willing to accept personal responsibility for their troubles, though, and for people like this, the Clubs are more of a dire admonition rather than a helpful suggestion.

Transformation is often challenging and painful, but it can strengthen us on multiple levels. The court cards in the suit of Clubs are people who have conquered challenges, people who are strong and often more experienced than you. They have risen from the ashes with more wisdom and resilience than they had before. These are people who can and often do prove to be valuable allies. They tend to be more sympathetic to your needs than are the people indicated by court cards in the other three suits. The Club court cards, unlike the numbered Clubs, do not point to transformation, but rather to people who have undergone transformation and are stronger for it.

Black and Red

As I mentioned earlier in this chapter, the Diamonds and Hearts lean toward stability (both material and emotional), while the Spades and Clubs tend to be cards of chaos and change. One of the first things I do when reading the cards, whether for myself or for someone else, is to see if there is an abundance of red or black cards. My definition of abundance varies by how many cards I am looking at, but at least 75 percent is a good rule of thumb. Thus, if I'm doing a simple three-card reading, all of the cards would have to be the same color to be an "abundance," whereas with a twelve-card spread, nine or more cards of the same color would catch my attention. An abundance of red or black cards can give you an immediate idea of whether the situation is relatively stable (mostly Diamonds and Hearts) or if it is fluid and changing (Spades and Clubs). The individual cards in the spread will then define the situation more clearly.

These elemental correspondences with the four suits are, of course, broad generalities. Their interpretation depends on multiple factors, and an abundance of cards of an opposing color can change almost any card's meaning. For example, the Seven of Hearts is sometimes called the marriage card because it indicates a stable and calm partnership of some kind. It is usually a good card to see in a reading. But if that same card is surrounded by an abundance of Spades and Clubs, it indicates that an already existing partnership may be threatened in some way.

Likewise, your own psychic impressions may conflict with these elemental generalities. When this happens, trust your instinct. What you bring to the table will and should affect your interpretations. The Seven of Hearts may speak to you of something other than emotional partnerships. Do not be afraid that you are just making up meanings when you interpret a card as indicating something other than what I describe in this book. That is exactly what you are doing, of course, but it is important to trust your intuition. In every deck ever used for divination, whether it is a deck of playing cards or Tarot cards or one of the many other decks that have been devised, the cards have meanings that *somebody made up*. You are the reader, so your insights are as valid as anyone else's, if not more so.

You may also see completely different interpretations of the cards if you read another book about divination with playing cards, and that is okay. I can only teach you the way I learned to read cards myself. I readily admit that there are other people who attribute different meanings to them. The important thing is that the cards reflect with reasonable accuracy the influences around you at the time you are reading them.

That said, you will find that the elemental associations given in this book can simplify the task of learning the divinatory meanings of playing cards. When you draw the Nine of Diamonds, you will instantly know it probably has something to do with money or material things or reputation, because that is the area of our existence that the suit of Diamonds represents. You will see emotional relationships when you draw Hearts, disruption or movement with Spades, and transformation of some kind when you draw a card from the suit of Clubs.

Now that you have finished this chapter, take up your deck of cards and shuffle through it, drawing cards at random. See and acknowledge each card's elemental correspondence. Even at this stage, a few of the cards may seem to have some meaning for you. Whether or not this happens is unimportant though. The purpose of this exercise is to become comfortable identifying your cards and how they reflect the four base elements of Earth, Water, Air, and Fire. As you look at a card, your mind should envision the concept of fortune, emotion, movement, or transformation, whichever is relevant to the card drawn.

Of course, the cards have more than four meanings! The elemental associations are just your first step. To gain an understanding of more specific interpretations, we will next look at numerology and how it applies to your interpretation when reading cards.

Three

Numerology and the Cards

Just as every card has an elemental influence, each of the pip cards (everything other than the court cards) is further defined by a number with its own influence.

Numerology is the study of the occult significance of numbers. It is believed that the philosopher Pythagoras once said, "The world is built upon the power of numbers." He theorized that everything in the universe can be conveyed numerically. In numerology, specific qualities are attributed to the numbers 1 through 9. Higher numbers are usually, but not always, reduced to a single digit by adding the digits together. (We'll look at reducing numbers more later in this chapter.) The Greeks considered the number 10 to be the "perfect" number because adding its digits together (1 + 0) cycled back to number 1. Numerologists convert names and dates to numbers and use these to make predictions and understand numerical influences. We will look at the basics of numerology in the latter part of this chapter, but for now, our interest is in how numerical influences apply to card reading.

Learning the significance of each playing card is so much easier when you see a numerological pattern from the Aces to the Tens. Combining this with an understanding of the elemental correspondences of the suits will give you a good idea of the essential meanings of the cards. In the four chapters following this one, we will examine the cards in more depth, one suit at a time, but for now, let us look at the patterns of the numbered sets.

It might help to look at your cards as we examine their numerological significance. Arrange your deck in order: Aces, Deuces, Threes, and so on, with the court cards (Kings, Queens, and Jacks) behind these. When you read about the Aces, look at each Ace card and think about how the number one influences that card's elemental correspondence. Continue to do this with all of your cards.

Also, refer to the appendix in the back of this book for keywords that will help you understand the numerological significance of the cards.

Numbered Cards (Pips)

The Aces

The word *ace* denotes a card or die with a single spot on it, but it has a secondary meaning similar to "best." Your best friend might be described as your ace, or you might say you aced a test if you did very well on it. The Aces are always emphatic and powerful when they appear in a reading.

An Ace is number one in every sense. The Aces are strong, aggressive cards that shout their elemental influences. In this way, they tend to have a more general meaning than other cards, being too forceful to indulge in complex nuances.

The Ace is always a triumphant card. Even in the mundane world, when people play card games the Aces usually have the highest value of all the cards, trumping even the Kings. When Aces appear in a reading, they have this same power. The message conveyed by an Ace may be further defined by the cards that fall around it, but its meaning is never overwhelmed or negated. This power card is almost always a good omen in any reading. It has a creative and independent quality.

The keyword for the Aces is *power*.

The Deuces

Two is a number of opposition and extremes. It is hot and cold, good and evil, high and low. The duality is not necessarily antagonistic, but a contrast is inherent in the Deuces. The appearance of these cards in a reading can be positive or negative, helpful or hurtful, or simultaneously both, because duality is the essential quality of the number two.

When you draw a Deuce, expect the unexpected. In card games the Deuces are often wild cards, and this may come from a subconscious recognition of their numerological significance. Deuces are also wild cards in a card reading. I have found them to be less connected to their respective elemental associations than other cards and more likely to influence the cards that appear next to them. If you would welcome an unexpected change, the Deuces can be nice to see in a reading.

Deuces can also indicate balance. This may seem like a contradiction, but it really isn't. Opposites have a tendency to cycle. Just as summer follows winter, an extreme situation will almost always eventually swing back in the other direction. This change is not something we intentionally plan, however, so the Deuces remain essentially wild cards even when they indicate a balancing influence. Deuces always indicate unexpected developments rather than anything that has been carefully planned out.

The keyword for the Deuces is *contrast*.

The Threes

With the Threes, the elemental associations become more important than with the Deuces, but they are nevertheless mellow influences. Three is a number of generation. Like seedlings, the Threes indicate a process of becoming, a promise for the future, rather than an end result in themselves. The elements clearly emerge when Threes appear in a reading. Here the elemental influences are tentative, and not always positive, even though they are clearly expressed. The Three of Diamonds is just a hint of Earth, a taste of success, which can be a disappointment if you were looking forward to a burst of good fortune.

Do not let this simplicity fool you. The significance of any Three card in a reading may not seem very important, but it can easily snowball into something more. Like a seedling, the situation or condition described by a Three card can grow into something much larger than it is now. In this way, a Three card can be a warning. On the other hand, when the Threes indicate something positive or helpful, they point to opportunities that can be cultivated and nurtured.

The Threes are cards of creativity. In a reading, they imply that careful thought will lead to pleasing or at least satisfactory results. The querent (the person whom the reading is for) usually has some control over the situation. Even when a Three card indicates something negative, it is rarely a permanent problem. It is a problem that can be overcome.

There is a timeless quality about a Three card related to the triangle as a symbol of past, present, and future. The Three card describes new events, but these are emerging from past actions. It is always speaking of something that has been around for a while, perhaps unnoticed, and will continue to be around unless the querent takes steps to change the situation.

The keyword for the Threes is *seedlings*.

The Fours

The number Four is steady and reliable, sometimes to the point of being stubborn. In card readings the Fours continue to express their elemental influence, but with more emphasis than the Threes and in a way that is less mutable. Changing the influence of a Four card can often be difficult for one reason or another. Of course, this same stubborn stability can be a blessing if the Four card indicates something you want to keep in your life.

There is a dull, ho-hum feeling to the Fours. This is not a bad thing, but these cards are not especially exciting. For example, the Four of Hearts speaks of emotional relationships; however, those emotions are not the heady, intoxicating feelings of romance and passion. This card indicates the more stable emotions of friendship. It could still speak of a romantic relationship, but this would be the calm and steady affection found in a long-term relationship. When a Four card appears in a reading, it indicates something low-key rather than fiery or erratic.

The lack of excitement is balanced by the endurance of the number four. Because of this endurance and stability, the naturally stable suits (Diamonds and Hearts) are especially positive when influenced by the number four. Unfortunately, under the influence of four, the naturally chaotic suits (Spades and Clubs) are almost always negative, although not disastrously so. Whatever the suit, when Fours appear in a reading, you can expect the situation to remain the same unless the querent takes active and persistent steps to create a change.

The keyword for the Fours is *stability*.

The Fives

The number five is the keystone number, with four numbers (1–4) before it and four numbers (6–9) following it. The Fives tend to be adventurous and unpredictable. In complete contrast to the Four cards, the number five has a quality of instability. This instability does not arise from contrast, as it does with the Deuces. Instead, there is more balance to it, but also a degree of uncertainty. The Fives represent change. As a very general rule, the red cards (Hearts and Diamonds) usually indicate a positive change, while the black cards (Clubs and Spades) are more often a negative change. But there are exceptions depending on your current situation and needs. Whether positive or negative, the change is always dynamic and forceful. There is nothing subtle about the Fives.

The Fives are the antithesis of routine. When these cards appear in a reading, you can expect something interesting to happen in your future. Keep in mind, though, the alleged curse "May you live in interesting times." Interesting is not always a good thing. With the chaotic suits of Spades and Clubs, the Five cards can be a little *too* interesting, warning of difficult times ahead. Sometimes boring and reliable is preferable, especially with a situation that you do not want to change. The Fives are reined in a little by the Diamonds and Hearts. In those suits, the Fives are generally safe as well as exciting.

Five is the number of our physical senses: touch, taste, sight, smell, and hearing. The Fives represent both sensuality and personal experiences. When a Five card comes up in a reading, it is speaking to the querent on a personal level, of things that are happening to the querent rather than to others around the person, although other people will often be involved. Whether positive or negative, these events are inevitably exciting on some level.

The keyword for the Fives is *dynamic.*

The Sixes

When we look at the Sixes, we find the exception to the rule concerning the relationship between numerology and cartomancy. From the perspective of numerology, the number six embodies the qualities of balance and dependability. It is a number of perfection, honesty, and satisfaction.

Not so from the perspective of cartomancy. The Sixes almost always have a negative meaning when they appear in a reading. A Six card indicates a weakening or interruption of the respective elemental influence. The Sixes are not tragic, but they are not especially desirable either. They represent a loss of some kind.

The good news—if anything about the Sixes can be described as good—is that they tend to describe temporary conditions. The appearance of a Six card indicates a setback rather than an absolute, irreversible failure. The Sixes speak of temporary disappointments.

The condition or situation indicated by a Six card cannot be entirely avoided because it is something that is already happening. With the more fluid, mutable suits of Spades and Clubs, this situation can often be altered by the querent, but the influence will still be felt. And whatever the suit of a Six card, the loss it describes will eventually correct itself or be forgotten entirely with the passage of time.

The keyword for the Sixes is *depletion*.

The Sevens

Seven is a number of completion and fulfillment. There are seven visible planets (using the original definition of *planet*, meaning a wandering celestial body), seven notes in a musical scale, and seven days of the week. In the Nine Herbs Charm, an old Anglo-Saxon healing spell, the herbs chervil and fennel are "sent into the Seven Worlds," meaning they are sent throughout all realms of existence. For followers of the Abrahamic religions, the biblical God created the world in seven days. Wherever we see the number seven, it symbolizes completion.

The Seven cards represent a fulfillment of their respective elemental associations. Not an excess and not a lack, it is a perfect completion. Like the Fours, the Sevens tend to accentuate the positive qualities of the Diamonds and Hearts and the negative qualities of Spades and Clubs.

Seven is also widely regarded as a magical number. Breaking a mirror brings bad luck for seven years. There are seven chakras, or energy centers, in the body.

Sevens in a card reading point to interpersonal situations. A Seven card does not indicate the querent alone, but rather the querent in relationship to at least one other person, if not more. Whether the situation is emotional, material, or transitional, a Seven card involves multiple people. The condition described by a Seven card may even affect the other person or people *more* than it affects the querent. There is almost always a social aspect like this to the Seven cards.

The keyword for the Sevens is *completion*.

The Eights

The number eight seizes the stability of four and takes it to the next level. Eight is a symbol of solidity and the material world. In numerology, it is the highest number that can be divided into two equal parts, then each of those numbers are divided again into two equal parts, and then each of those are once again divided equally—showing a stable balance with each division. Due to its association with the physical world, the number eight often represents material or financial success.

Eight is a number of manifestation. In the Wiccan religion, the year is celebrated with eight seasonal sabbats. For Christians, the biblical God spared eight men and women on Noah's ark. Buddhism has its eightfold path to nirvana.

In a card reading, an Eight card indicates its respective elemental influence manifesting in the querent's life. Whatever that influence might be, it always involves the physical, material world. There is nothing subtle about the Eights. An Eight is usually a good card to see, as it speaks of potential opportunities for the querent.

The Eight cards are a step forward. They do not concern themselves with what was, but rather with what will be. An Eight card always indicates a future event, not something distant, and it is usually an event or situation that will arise in the very near future.

The keyword for the Eights is *manifestation*.

The Nines

Nine is a number of wisdom and magic. The Great Ennead is a group of nine gods and goddesses who were worshipped in the Egyptian city of Heliopolis. In ancient Greece, the nine Muses governed the arts and sciences and filled mortals with inspiration. Nine is a number of spiritual awakening. As the final and greatest single-digit number, it is symbolic of the end of a cycle.

In card readings, the Nines are often indicative of wisdom in one way or another. If the Nine card is a Diamond or Heart, wisdom will protect that respective aspect of the querent's life. In the Spade and Club suits, a Nine card indicates the opposite: a lack of wisdom that can result in surprising and perhaps unpleasant results.

When a Nine card appears, you (or the querent, if this is someone other than yourself) may feel that the situation is beyond your control. However, the Nines speak of conditions that either you have created or you can avert or alter by your own actions. Remember, the Sevens represent completion, whereas the Nines represent cycles. The Nine cards show evolving situations. Whatever is happening, it isn't the end result, but rather is a process of change. In this respect, there is a similarity between the Nines and the Threes.

The keyword for the Nines is *wisdom*.

The Tens

In numerology, all numbers with more than one digit are reduced to a single digit by adding those digits together, repeating this until the result is a number between 1 and 9. (We'll look more at reducing numbers later in this chapter.) When we add the two digits of the number 10 (1 + 0), the result is 1.

It should come as no surprise then that there are similarities between the four Ten cards and the four Aces. Like the Aces, the Tens are aggressive cards. By that I mean they express their respective elemental influences explicitly and without apology.

How are the Tens different? Unlike the Aces, the Tens rarely if ever have the highest value in card games; the Tens are trumped not only by the Aces but also by the three court cards. The Ten card is always forceful, but it is not necessarily triumphant, at least as far as the querent is concerned. Depending on what you want out of life, a Ten card isn't even necessarily good. As you might expect, the Ten of Hearts and Ten of Diamonds are both wonderful cards to see in a reading. This is not necessarily true, though, for the Ten of Clubs, and certainly not for the Ten of Spades. When a Ten card comes up in a reading, look at the cards surrounding it to get a better idea of how the situation will affect the querent.

The keyword for the Tens is *force*.

Court Cards

Let us step away from numerology for now as we look at the court cards: the Jack, the Queen, and the King. An understanding of numerology will not help you with these cards, but the significance of each court card is easy to learn.

Court cards are also called face cards because they depict human faces. Although they are influenced by elemental associations like the other cards in your deck, court cards almost always represent people.

The Kings

The Kings often represent mature males; however, the definition of "mature" can vary depending on the age of the querent. This is because our perspective changes as we age. For younger people, the Kings represent people who are older and more experienced. However, if the querent is forty or older, a King can represent almost any person who is also forty or older, regardless of whether that person is older than the querent. Forty is admittedly a generalization, but by this age most people have settled into established patterns that will stay with them for the rest of their lives. This doesn't mean there will be no changes in their lives. My own life changed considerably when I began writing in my fifties, but my writing is based on decades of well-established life patterns.

Keep in mind, too, that the concepts of masculine and feminine are cultural constructs. While the Kings tend to indicate men, a King in your reading can refer to anyone fulfilling a traditionally "male" archetype. The King is the warrior, the protector, the provider, regardless of gender.

The Queens

The four Queens, as you might expect, often represent mature females. As with the King cards, the definition of a Queen can vary according to the age of the querent. Queens are mature, experienced women. A Queen card could indicate the querent's mother or grandmother, but not a daughter, even if that daughter is forty or older. Kings and Queens are people we look up to, or at the very least look to as peers. As with the Kings, Queens can refer to someone of a specific gender, but they can also indicate any person fulfilling a traditionally "female" archetype, such as the homemaker, the nurturer, and the healer.

The Jacks

The Jacks usually represent younger, less mature people, regardless of their gender or the archetypal role they play in the reading. These are, however, people who influence you, so a Jack rarely indicates a child, unless it is your own child and biologically an adult. For querents over the age of forty, the Jacks usually represent younger people. Otherwise, the Jack could indicate someone your own age but less experienced. If the querent is extremely young, someone in their early teens, then a Jack could even indicate an actual child.

✦ ✦ ✦

The court cards are people who can influence us directly through their actions and decisions. Further distinctions are a matter of perspective and will vary from one individual to another. It is up to the reader to determine how one of these cards should be interpreted. The interpretation will vary depending on who you are and who you are reading for.

Basic Numerology

I mentioned earlier in this chapter that in numerology we "reduce" multiple-digit numbers by adding the digits together and repeating the process until the result is a single digit between 1 and 9. As an example, 297 is reduced by adding $2 + 9 + 7$. The sum is 18, which is further reduced by adding $1 + 8$, for a final sum of 9.

The exceptions to this are the numbers 11 and 22, which many numerologists consider "master numbers" and do not reduce further. I have heard different reasons for this, but in any event, there are no 11s or 22s in a deck of playing cards, so these master numbers are irrelevant for our purposes. I mention them here merely as an item of interest.

Every person has several numbers that a numerologist might use to make predictions or gain insights about that person's character. The first of these is your birth number, sometimes referred to as your destiny number. To calculate your birth number, simply add up all of the digits in your birth date (month, day, and year) and reduce the sum as I have described here until you have a single-digit result. Thus, someone born on April Fools' Day in the year 2000 would add 4 (the month) + 1 (the day) + 2 + 0 + 0 + 0 (for the year), with a result of 7, which, of course, does not need to be reduced further.

The birth number represents inherent traits and is unalterable. You also have at least one name number. This is the character you develop and present to others. One person may have several name numbers, although one will be the primary name they are known by. Alice Smith, for example, may marry Robert Jones and thereafter (if she takes his surname) be known as Alice Jones. But marriage is not the only reason a person might have a name change, or even multiple names. Samuel Clemens was better known as Mark Twain. And witches often adopt magical names both to represent their new lives and as a means of protection from others who would inflict harm on them. There are many reasons why people change their names. We are concerned here with your most authentic name, the name that the greatest number of people in your life know you by. This is not necessarily the same name as the one on your birth certificate.

To calculate your name number, use the name you use in everyday life. Jaqueline Anne Thomas probably does not use her full name anywhere other than on legal documents. (My apologies to anyone whose name actually is Jaqueline Anne Thomas, especially if this is how you present yourself to others.) More likely she is Jackie Thomas to most people. Or maybe, for some personal reason, she goes by Anne Thomas. If she is a witch, she may even use another name entirely, like Silver or Isis or Rhiannon, especially if most of the people she interacts with are also part of the magical community. Your most authentic name is the one that people most often call you. It is the name that you are usually known by.

To calculate your name number, it is first necessary to convert each letter in your name to a number, which you can do with the following table:

1	2	3	4	5	6	7	8	9
A	B	C	D	E	F	G	H	I
J	K	L	M	N	O	P	Q	R
S	T	U	V	W	X	Y	Z	

After doing this, add all of the numbers together and reduce the total until you have a single-digit number. *Alaric Albertsson* is converted to a name number as shown here:

$$(1 + 3 + 1 + 9 + 9 + 3) + (1 + 3 + 2 + 5 + 9 + 2 + 1 + 1 + 6 + 5) = 61$$
$$6 + 1 = 7$$

If you know your birth number and name number, you may find that one of the cards takes on a special meaning as "your" card. Your card's suit will be whichever suit corresponds to the predominant element in your natal horoscope. When I was born, the Sun, Moon, Mercury, Saturn, and Ascendant were all in water signs. Water, of course, corresponds to the suit of Hearts. Seven happens to be both my birth number and my name number. When I am reading the cards for myself, the Seven of Hearts often represents "me." You may find that one of the cards indicates you in the same way, but let your intuition guide you. The number of your personal card could be the same as either your birth number or your name number, although the latter is more likely.

And as I said, some people have more than one name number. One of these numbers, the one that corresponds to the name they use most often, is their most authentic name number, but in certain situations another name number may be more appropriate. Jackie Thomas is a 7, but if Jackie is a witch who uses the name Silver, then the number 4 of the appropriate suit might be the card she would use for questions relating specifically to her relationship with other witches and occultists. Of course, if her magical name includes a surname, like the well-known authors Silver RavenWolf and Oberon Zell, then the entire name would be reduced to a number.

If you read cards for other people, you probably do not want to calculate numbers for each of your querents, nor is there any need to do so if you only read for that person once in a while. However, if you give frequent readings for someone close to you, perhaps a good friend or family member, then you might want to calculate that person's birth and name numbers and see if a particular card manifests as the querent's personal card.

Try It for Yourself

Now go back to your deck of cards again. Shuffle the deck and draw cards at random, noting the elemental influence and the number of each card. When you draw the Six of Diamonds, you should think of *depletion* (the number six) + *fortune* (Diamonds). The Nine of Clubs should make you think of *wisdom* (the number nine) + *transformation* (Clubs). As you do this, some of these paired concepts may take on a special meaning. That is great! It means the cards are beginning to speak to you.

For the most part, you should trust your intuition, but the card meanings will usually follow the pattern of elements and numbers that I have described thus far. If more than a few cards diverge from this, make sure your intuition is not being derailed by your personal biases. For someone who is young and single, every card may seem to indicate romance. A person focused on health issues may see dire (or optimistic) medical implications in most of the cards. If a lot of cards seem to have interpretations that diverge from the elemental and numerological correspondences described here, especially if your interpretations have a common theme, then it could be the result of your biases rather than real psychic insight. The trick is to keep your mind clear and open without letting your imagination take you on a joy ride.

We have examined the elemental influences of the four suits and the numerological significance of each numbered card. With just this knowledge and nothing more, you can begin to practice reading cards. If you would like to do so, skip ahead to chapter 8 and learn how to lay out the cards for a reading. And if your results are less than satisfactory, if *completion + movement* (Seven of Spades) means nothing to you, don't despair! In the following four chapters, we will look at specific interpretations of the cards one suit at a time.

Four

The Suit of Diamonds

When reading cards, the Diamonds represent material fortune, influence, and reputation. Essentially, they speak of things that we often associate, at least indirectly, with diamonds.

The suit of Diamonds reflects the cool, dry element of Earth. Throughout most of history, diamonds were valuable largely because they were so hard to find. This changed in the 1800s when extensive diamond mines were discovered in South Africa; however, diamonds are still widely regarded as a symbol of wealth and luxury. Diamond is one of the hardest known substances in the world, which also contributes to its perceived value. In the first decks of European playing cards, the Diamonds were represented as a suit of Coins, a symbol still used in some Tarot decks.

But whether a diamond or a coin, this is still merely a symbol. Other cultures had their own symbols of material prosperity. In northern Europe, wealth was more often measured in cattle and land than in stones or metal disks. Gemstones and precious metals were valued, of course, but they were things that could be obtained with wealth rather than being symbols of wealth itself. There are many things that can be symbols for the abstract concept of wealth. This is important to keep in mind because the suit of Diamonds represents fortune, but this does not necessarily mean money as we think of it in our culture.

Diamonds can even refer to your physical condition, since a healthy body is certainly a fortunate asset.

Ace of Diamonds

Power + Fortune

When this card appears in a reading, expect a burst of good fortune. There is nothing secretive or subtle about the Ace of Diamonds, so it can be "negative" if it addresses an event or situation that you don't want others to know about. Otherwise, this is a good card to see.

The good fortune represented by the Ace of Diamonds could very well be financial in nature, but this card is just as likely to indicate your reputation or some other asset unrelated to money. Ultimately, the Ace of Diamonds is a good luck card. If that luck involves your finances, it will be a windfall. If it's your reputation, you will gain notable prestige. ("You" refers to the querent, of course. It only means you in a literal sense if you are reading the cards for yourself.) Whenever and wherever the card manifests in a reading, the Ace of Diamonds is luck.

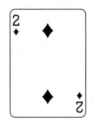

Two of Diamonds

Contrast + Fortune

This card is less influenced by its suit than the other Diamonds are. It indicates a surprise of some kind, an unexpected event or outcome. Look to the cards that fall next to the Two of Diamonds. If those cards are also Diamonds, that is where the surprise will come from; it will be something involving money or your reputation. Otherwise, if the Deuce isn't near any other fortune cards, the nature of the surprise could be almost anything. The Two of Diamonds breaks apart the old order to make way for the new.

The change spoken of by the Two of Diamonds may be pleasant or unpleasant, but it is never catastrophic. If there are no other Deuces next to this card, it indicates a small change. When the Two of Diamonds falls next to one or more other Deuces, expect a wild ride! The Deuces are the wild cards in your deck.

Three of Diamonds

Seedlings + Fortune

Fortune is expressing itself when this card appears, but in a very mild way. There is some potential for fortune or luck; however, this has not come into full manifestation. Patience is called for.

The Three of Diamonds is often a warning. It means "no, not now." The card can be telling you to stop and consider your actions carefully. You may see a glimmer of luck, but the time is not right yet for whatever it is you intend to do. In reference to finances, this card is telling you to spend cautiously and to be wary of making any investments. Luck, however, can take many forms. If you are in a new relationship, the Three of Diamonds is warning you not to take the commitment any further at this time. If you are thinking about moving out of state, think again. Wait.

However, this is not really a bad card to see in a reading. Three is the number of expression, so don't interpret the card as "never ever." Instead, it is saying "not right now," "not yet." Remember that the keyword for the Threes is seedlings. Young seedlings emerging from the soil hold some promise, perhaps a bountiful crop of vegetables or maybe colorful flowers. But if you dig up those seedlings now, there will never be a harvest.

Occasionally the Three of Diamonds will indicate a temporary illness. Essentially, your body is saying "no," forcing you to slow down for a while.

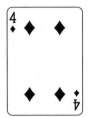

Four of Diamonds

Stability + Fortune

Coupling fortune with stability gives us a card for success! The potential slumbering in the Three of Diamonds has found its footing in the Four. There is no longer any need to wait; what you are hoping for is going to happen.

I have heard the Four of Diamonds described as the insurance card. What it guarantees, of course, is stability. Thus, it does not indicate any drastic change in your life. The success you achieve, in whatever form it is taking, is a manifestation of something that was already present rather than something coming at you from out of the blue. In the financial arena, it could indicate that you will be receiving a deserved raise or that your investments are secure. If the card is referencing your reputation, people will see you for who you are despite any gossip going around. It can indicate good health.

The Four of Diamonds can also signify understanding and an ability to control the situation around you. It speaks of your own stability and reliability in relationship to the world around you.

Five of Diamonds

Dynamic + Fortune

This is an exciting card. When the Five of Diamonds appears in a reading, expect the unexpected! Something unforeseen is going to happen, usually in a good way. Your plans are going to work out better than you had expected.

Just as the Four of this suit is sometimes described as an insurance card, I have heard the Five of Diamonds called the destiny card. This is because it foretells something beyond your control, a sort of happy accident. Something is going to happen that you did not plan on, although the event could enhance your current plans in some way. The Five of Diamonds is almost always a cheerful card when it appears in a reading.

How could this card possibly have a negative connotation? Well, it could be negative if you do not want any changes in your life. Change can be frightening for some people. And even good, productive changes do not always seem good and productive at the time.

The Fives speak to us on a personal level, so this unexpected stroke of fortune is something that will happen specifically to the querent. It isn't something that will happen to the querent's entire family or to a club or an organization that the querent belongs to. Others may benefit indirectly, but this card indicates a personal event.

Six of Diamonds

Depletion + Fortune

As you might guess, the Six of Diamonds indicates a loss of money. Unlike other cards in the suit of Diamonds, the Six almost always indicates either money or reputation rather than luck or health. This financial loss or damaged reputation is usually neither chronic nor disastrous, and in that sense the Six of Diamonds can sometimes be a "good" card to see. A temporary monetary setback is far preferable to financial ruin! Look at the cards that fall next to this one. The Six of Diamonds falling next to the Ten of Spades actually *could* mean financial ruin. If it is next to any of the Diamond court cards, somebody might be speaking ill of you behind your back.

Very often, the loss—whether it is money or reputation—is brought on by a single, finite incident. The card can indicate misplaced cash or something like a lost receipt for reimbursement or a tax deduction. It can be an embarrassing incident that tarnishes your reputation for a while but is eventually forgotten.

This is rarely a prediction of something that can be averted. Often the loss has already taken place, even though the querent may not be aware of it. If not, then events leading up to the loss have already transpired. In any event, the querent has experienced either a financial loss or a loss of reputation, or will see one of these in the near future.

Seven of Diamonds

Completion + Fortune

While the Six of Diamonds indicates a loss of money or reputation, the Seven indicates a gain. That's the good news, but there's one catch: it isn't your gain. A Seven card always indicates some kind of relationship, and for the Seven of Diamonds it means a gain for a person close to you. That lucky person could be a friend, a relative, a spouse, or even a business partner.

The gain is in some manifestation of fortune that may or may not be financial in nature. It could be an improved reputation or just a lucky break. If it is a monetary gain, this will not be extravagant. Seven is a number of completion, not overwhelming abundance. Whatever form it takes, this gain will be a pleasant surprise for the recipient, something they may have hoped for but did not really expect.

Although the Seven of Diamonds represents somebody else's gain, it is possible that the querent could nevertheless benefit indirectly from it, especially if the lucky recipient is the querent's spouse or business partner. But the querent's benefit, if any, will be a collateral effect. The primary beneficiary will be someone else in the querent's life.

Eight of Diamonds
Manifestation + Fortune

The manifestation of fortune means that the querent can expect positive, uplifting events in the near future. These events could be financial in nature, but in my experience they are more often something less tangible. They do, however, involve the physical world. If the event is an improved relationship with somebody, the change will result in very real benefits for the querent. Like the Four of Diamonds, the Eight can indicate improved health. Think of the Eight of Diamonds as the querent's good luck card, although not in the dramatic way seen with the Ace of Diamonds. The events predicted by this card are not life-changing; however, they may present an opportunity for greater achievement. This might seem like a good time for the querent to make a grab for that brass ring, but they should do so only if it is clearly within reach.

When the Eight of this suit speaks of a financial change, it will be something steady but not overwhelming. The Eight of Diamonds indicates a good time to begin or focus on saving money. This is not a time for the querent to indulge in speculative financial ventures. Investments should be solid and reliable. If this card is speaking of your reputation, it is a good time to expand your connections and influence.

Nine of Diamonds

Wisdom + Fortune

When the Nine of Diamonds appears in a reading, it tells you that your fortune is secure and protected. Very often fortune means your finances, but as is so often the case with this suit, it can also indicate your reputation, your nonmonetary assets, your health, or anything else that might be construed as "fortune."

This protection does not mean you can act foolishly or frivolously. Your actions will still have a direct influence on your fortune. The Nine of Diamonds indicates that it will be relatively easy for you to make the right choices. Nevertheless, it is your responsibility to make *intelligent* choices to the best of your ability. Let your wisdom guide you. This is a time of change, so the end result of those choices may not be immediately apparent.

While the Eight of this suit speaks of future events, the Nine of Diamonds reflects events that are already unfolding. This card tells you to stay the course and trust that your fortune is protected.

Ten of Diamonds

Force + Fortune

The Ten of Diamonds indicates that the querent will either receive a substantial amount of money or experience an unexpected rise in popularity. This is always a notable event; however, the exact amount of money or popularity depends on the querent's current circumstances. "Substantial" and "rise" are, of course, relative terms. If the querent is broke, then fifty dollars might seem like a substantial fortune, but the same sum will be insignificant to many other people.

This sudden surge of fortune can have collateral effects that the querent may or may not desire. The substantial amount of money, for example, may come in the form of a fantastic job offer that will require the querent to relocate to another state. Usually, however, the Ten of this suit is a very good card to see in a reading.

The other downside to the Ten of Diamonds is that it is a temporary boon. Unlike the Ace, Eight, or Nine of this suit, the Ten of Diamonds does not speak of long-term gains. It is a one-shot thing. The rise in popularity could disappear next month. The money gained is probably going to be something that the querent will spend and enjoy, not something that will grow over time. Like the Ace of this suit, the Ten of Diamonds represents a burst of good fortune, but its long-term effects will depend on the querent's decisions and actions.

Jack of Diamonds

If you are forty or older, a Jack indicates someone younger than you. If you are under forty, the card can sometimes indicate a person your own age or even older, but that person is someone you perceive as less experienced or mature than you.

The Jack of Diamonds is a person with a friendly, comfortable demeanor. This person is also ambitious, which may or may not be a good thing. They may have an agenda that is not easy to discern. It could represent someone new to your place of employment who covets your position.

While the Jack of Diamonds is usually a cautionary card in a reading, it does not necessarily mean that the person in question is irredeemably bad. Your Jack (or Jill) may be a basically decent person but nevertheless have hidden goals or desires that conflict with your own. The card is telling you to watch for a younger or less mature person. You don't have to avoid this person, but be careful of how much trust you extend to them. Caution may not be as important if you are secure in your position, whether in your career or simply in your social arena. In the right circumstances, a younger ambitious person can be a good ally.

Queen of Diamonds

The Queens indicate mature people, and the Queen of Diamonds is often a person with secrets. Like the Jack of this suit, she is probably ambitious and her secret is likely a part of some covert agenda. Although she is mature, her age is not revealed by the card. For younger querents, this card represents an older woman or an older person who fulfills a traditionally feminine archetype. If the querent is forty or older, however, this person could be younger than the querent, but she is someone whom the querent nevertheless perceives as a peer.

This person's secrets may involve some issue that the querent is in on. This card is about deceit, but it may not be the querent who is being deceived. However, if the querent is not aware of the secret, then this card is a warning that things are not exactly as they seem. The querent should watch for somebody who may be hiding something. As with the Jack of this suit, when the Queen of Diamonds appears in a reading, the querent does not necessarily have to avoid this person entirely but should just be careful in interactions with them for now. Also, as with the Jack, in some situations the person may be an ally.

King of Diamonds

The King of this suit is the masculine counterpart of the Queen. The King of Diamonds indicates an adult, often one in a position of power due to his wealth or reputation, or both. He will have a dignified demeanor.

This person has some hidden or secret agenda, but as with all of the Diamond court cards, be careful how you interpret this. Look for clarification in other cards that fall near this King. The secret may be something you need to worry about. It could even be a secret that you're in on. In fact, *you* could be the King's secret!

If all of this seems a mystery, if you are not aware of someone with a secret, then watch for a man who seems congenial and dignified. He has some plan or secret that may be contrary to your own goals. Let your intuition guide you when any of the Diamond court cards appear in a reading.

Five

The Suit of Hearts

The suit of Hearts reflects the cool, moist element of Water. Modern anatomical medicine defines the heart as a muscle that causes blood to circulate throughout the body, but historically the heart was perceived as the seat of our emotions (possibly because it beats faster and harder when we are excited). People "give their hearts" to those they love, and those hearts are "broken" if that love is not honored and returned. An emotion of almost any kind is described as "heartfelt" if it is deep and sincere.

The symbol of the heart is often associated with valentines and romantic love, with sexual relationships, passion, and infatuation. But emotions come in an array of sizes and flavors. Sorrow is an emotion. Cold fury is an emotion. The cards of the Heart suit reveal the querent's general emotional state, but they do not indicate how those emotions are manifesting. Look to surrounding cards for clarification when Hearts appear in your reading. Also, consider the querent's age and current lifestyle when interpreting the Hearts. For a younger, single querent, a card from this suit is very likely to indicate romantic affection, whereas for older querents and especially those in stable, long-term relationships, the Hearts are more likely to speak of familial or platonic emotions.

Ace of Hearts

Power + Emotion

The Aces express general but powerful concepts. When you see the Ace of Hearts, expect a surge of love. It may indicate romance, but if so, the emphasis is on the emotional aspect rather than the physical, sexual aspect. The love may spring up from within you or it may come from someone else, but in either case it will be strong and prevailing.

This can be a very social card, involving not just one other person but your entire circle of friends. Here the affection is more dispersed, but the card indicates a notable improvement in your social life. This is a good time to pursue and nurture your emotional relationships with others. In this interpretation, too, there may be some romance in these relationships if you are at a stage in your life where you are open to such things. But again, this card speaks of positive emotional connections between you and others, whether or not there is any sexual element involved. Platonic friendship is an emotional bond, too. The Ace of Hearts is love, whether romantic or not.

Two of Hearts

Contrast + Emotion

The Deuces are always wild cards, indicating something unexpected. For the Two of Hearts, this is often a pleasant surprise. Like other Deuces, this card influences the cards that fall around it and should be interpreted in that context. When the Two of Hearts appears next to another Heart card, it can indicate nice but unexpected changes in your social life. Next to a Diamond card, it may indicate a gift or recommendation from someone close to you.

There are some configurations where the Two of Hearts may be a warning. If it falls next to any of the Diamond court cards, be wary, for the surprise may be a gift, but it could also be something you will not appreciate. For that matter, any surprise may be undesirable for people who always want their lives to be structured and well-ordered. As a rule, though, the Two of Hearts is usually a nice card to see in a reading.

Three of Hearts
Seedlings + Emotion

With the Three of Hearts, the querent's emotions gently manifest in a positive and pleasant way. This card represents simple pleasures such as hobbies and leisure activities. Whatever the pastime, it is an activity that is familiar and comfortable for the querent. These activities are seedlings of pleasure. They are not end results in themselves, but rather activities that lead us to a contented existence.

Therefore, the pleasures that the Three of Hearts speaks of are enjoyable but not mind-blowing. This is not a trip to Disney World, unless the querent happens to live in Orlando and makes semi-regular visits to the resort. This card indicates *simple* pleasures, and this varies from one person to another. What I find to be a simple pleasure might be a new and exciting experience for you, and vice versa. In contrast to the wild Deuce, when the Three of Hearts appears, the querent is in control.

If this card falls next to the Nine of Spades, the querent may need to develop a more responsible attitude about leisure activities. Usually, though, the Three of Hearts is a positive card to see in a reading. It counsels the querent to pursue hobbies and pleasant activities, especially those that provide a creative outlet.

Four of Hearts

Stability + Emotion

I think of this as the friendship card. The Four of Hearts brings a constancy to your emotional relationships wherever it appears in a reading. This card can sometimes be related to romance, but only in an indirect way. If you have been dating somebody for a while, for example, the Four of Hearts could indicate that the other person will soon be ready to settle into a more permanent relationship with you.

More often, though, the Four of Hearts is speaking about friendly, non-romantic relationships. This can involve your social circle, but it could just as easily indicate warm relationships in your workplace or with family members.

Like the Four of Diamonds, this is almost always a positive card to see in a reading. The Four of Hearts is a good card to see in a reading even if you are an introvert, because the relationships it predicts are unlikely to be overwhelming for you. The relationships it describes are low-key but nevertheless fulfilling. I suppose if you are hoping a relationship will erupt into something wild and passionate, then it would be disappointing to see the Four of Hearts, but in most circumstances it is nice to have this card come up.

Five of Hearts

Dynamic + Emotion

The Five of Hearts is a card that shakes things up. It is a card that breaks routine but almost always in a good way.

If the Four of Hearts is the friendship card, then the Five is the party card. The Five of Hearts predicts fun, exciting, and certainly interesting events in the querent's future.

If the querent is single, the Five of Hearts can be a very romantic card, hinting at flirtations and fun, sensual connections. This is not a card to look for if the querent is seeking a long-term relationship, however. It is possible that the querent's fun first date could eventually lead to something more lasting, but the Five of Hearts promises only momentary pleasure, nothing more.

For introverts, the Five of Hearts is not always a great card to see in a reading. There is a very strong social aspect to this card, and not everyone is comfortable with that. And even if you thoroughly enjoy the company of others, there are times when parties and flirtations are more of a distraction than anything else.

This could also be a cautionary card if the querent is in any form of long-term relationship where outside flirtations and trysts would be undesirable. The Five of Hearts is usually a positive card, though. For many people, its presence predicts fun and entertaining connections of a platonic (but no less exciting) nature. However it manifests, it is always a very social card.

Six of Hearts

Depletion + Emotion

When we lose the warmth and comfort of affection, what remains is not just an absence, but a disturbed and disrupted emotional condition. This is what you can expect when the Six of Hearts appears in a reading: anger, grief, arguments. This card predicts emotional turbulence.

The imminent emotional conflict is not something that will spring out of nowhere. The situation or conditions behind it are already in motion and may have existed for some time. If your partner is cheating on you, or vice versa, the indiscretion will soon come to light. Or perhaps some growing resentment between you and a friend or sibling will erupt in an open confrontation. Whatever it is that will upset you, it is already going on, so the best you can do is brace yourself for the impact.

This emotional disturbance will not last forever, but it could have permanent consequences. When the Six of Hearts appears in a reading, it might be a good idea to avoid making any decisions or saying anything that you might regret later.

Seven of Hearts

Completion + Emotion

This is sometimes called the marriage card, and for good reason. The Seven of Hearts predicts emotional completion and fulfillment. It is the happily ever after at the end of every romance novel.

The Seven of Hearts can predict a coming marriage, but it often simply refers to a marriage that already exists. Likewise, this card can be referring either to the querent's marriage or to someone else's marriage. Look at the cards that fall near the Seven of Hearts and listen closely to your intuition.

Keep in mind, too, that this card speaks of true marriage. A marriage is an ongoing, committed relationship between two people. While a marriage may be reflected in a symbolic ceremony, the wedding itself does not create the relationship, nor does a government-issued license (or the lack thereof) affect the relationship in any way beyond whatever legal rights that license may grant or deny. The Seven of Hearts describes the calm and serene relationship between two souls who have grown comfortable with each other over a period of time.

This card will sometimes indicate non-romantic (but non-familial) relationships as well, such as a deep friendship that is not in any way sexual, although that is really more the domain of the Eight of Hearts. The Seven of Hearts is another very social card, though, and always describes some kind of fulfilling union with another person or persons.

Eight of Hearts
Manifestation + Emotion

The Eight of Hearts combines the material nature of the number eight with the emotions inherent in the suit of Hearts. It predicts that you will gain something of value through love or affection. Perhaps you will be getting a raise, not only for the work you have done but also because your boss likes you. Or you may be receiving a gift given out of affection by a relative or friend. Something is coming to you, or some opportunity is opening up, because of how others feel about you.

Expect friendly reactions from those around you. The Eight of Hearts will not tell you exactly when you will receive the opportunity or gift, but it will come in the near future.

This card can also indicate improved business activity if you sell or provide something that inspires love and attraction between people. This includes an array of goods and services such as perfume sales, computer dating, or sexy lingerie sales. If you are selling "love," the Eight of Hearts can be describing your work, but usually the card is predicting some kind of gift or gain due to the feelings that one or more other people have for you. The gift is not always a tangible item, but could be something like an offer of assistance, for example.

Nine of Hearts

Wisdom + Emotion

The Nine of Hearts is the querent's protection card. Whereas the Nine of Diamonds indicates a protected reputation or financial interests, the Nine of Hearts is a more general, all-encompassing protection. When this card appears in a reading, the querent is in control of the situation and with little effort should be able to make wise decisions leading to the desired outcome.

In this way, the Nine of Hearts can be thought of as a good luck card, but it really is not luck at all since the outcome will be the result of the querent's own actions. The card indicates that the querent has the wisdom to choose the right actions to take.

The protection indicated here is very personal. Think of the Nine of Hearts as saying the querent's heart is protected. The querent may even experience a deep sense of spiritual joy. This protection, this joy, is not so much an event as it is an evolving process that will somehow lead the querent in a new direction.

Ten of Hearts

Force + Emotion

The Ten of Hearts indicates strong, overwhelming feelings of emotional attraction—which may or may not be a good thing. In the right circumstances, this can be a wonderful card to see in a reading. The Ten of Hearts represents complete fulfillment, a level of joy so intense that it catches your breath. Think of your first adolescent crush, when new and passionate feelings swept over you. This card predicts the kind of rush of emotion that can affect your every thought.

Usually the Ten of Hearts is a positive card, but its very force can sometimes lead to an undesirable end. In romance, its intensity can actually sabotage a relationship, frightening off the other party, so in this way it can be a cautionary card. It could also be a warning that intense emotions will be a distraction for you. If you can remain in control of your thoughts and actions, though, you can expect an exhilarating emotional ride.

Bear in mind that the emotions expressed by the Ten of Hearts will not necessarily be sensual or romantic in nature. An ecstatic spiritual experience can be as powerful as any sexual feelings. The Ten of Hearts often speaks of romance, but it really can indicate any kind of deep emotion. It is that sense of complete fulfillment.

Jack of Hearts

The suit of Hearts shamelessly breaks the "age rule" regarding Jacks, Queens, and Kings. The Jack of Hearts can be anybody of any age. The defining quality here is that it is a person who has been in the querent's life for a while. This is not a new person in the querent's life or someone the querent has yet to meet.

The Jack of Hearts is also a person with whom the querent has a significant emotional relationship, as you might expect with the suit of Hearts. The nature of the relationship is not always romantic; the card could mean a lover or spouse, but it could just as easily be a family member, a longtime friend, or even a coworker. There is an emotional connection of some kind, though. The Jack of Hearts would not indicate someone who just happens to live down the street from the querent unless they both are involved with each other on some level, even if the other person is someone the querent sees in passing several times a week.

Whatever the nature of the relationship indicated by this card, the Jack of Hearts is someone with whom the querent has a positive, meaningful rapport.

Queen of Hearts

Like the other court cards of this suit, the Queen of Hearts is not so much indicative of age as of function. This Queen can be any age, but she is a person with some experience. This is not someone you perceive as childish. This card may represent a person you do not yet know but will soon meet. If it is someone you already know, your relationship with them will be changing, moving to a deeper and more intimate level.

If your sexual preference is for women, then this card may speak of romance. The Queen of Hearts can be a very passionate card. If you are not attracted to women, the card can still represent a female you have a connection with, perhaps a relative or friend.

If this interpretation does not feel right to you, if it goes against your intuition, then perhaps the card has another meaning entirely. Sometimes the Queen of Hearts simply indicates passion in general, regardless of your gender or that of the other party. Always go with your intuition when interpreting the Queen of Hearts.

King of Hearts

This card is essentially the masculine version of the Queen of Hearts. The King of Hearts represents a person of any age whom the querent perceives as having some experience and maturity. This person is probably a laid-back, easygoing individual. Very often the card represents a person the querent will soon meet. If the querent already knows this person, then the relationship will be changing and evolving.

If the querent is not attracted to men sexually, then the King of Hearts represents a friend or close associate. Here again, it may be somebody the querent has not yet met. The card predicts a change in relationship, which could be the start of a new relationship or the evolution of an existing one.

Six

The Suit of Spades

The Spades represent the warm, moist element of Air. Almost unnoticeable when still and calm, air becomes a force to reckon with when it is set into motion. The motion of the air is often useful and most welcome. Since the dawn of time, a gentle breeze has brought relief to both human and beast on hot summer days. We humans eventually learned to harness the wind to carry our carracks and caravels across the waves. Today we know the motion of air could provide much, if not all, of our electrical power thanks to the development of efficient wind turbines.

But moving air can also be discouraging or even destructive. Under the right conditions, those winds that propel a sailboat can gather strength out at sea and build into a hurricane, demolishing buildings and threatening lives when it reaches the coastline. Farther inland, in North America, tornadoes often rip across the plains east of the Rocky Mountains. When air is set into motion, it very often creates adversarial conditions for us. This is reflected in the suit of Spades. Some cards in this suit indicate that you have the wind at your back, but others predict difficulties.

In the oldest decks of playing cards and still in some Tarot decks today, the suit of Spades was represented as swords. The symbolism of a sword, too, can represent situations that are either empowering or threatening; it just depends on which end of the weapon you are dealing with.

Ace of Spades

Power + Movement

The Ace of Spades is a card of conquest. The querent may be facing obstacles, perhaps severe obstacles, but will ultimately succeed in the end. This card predicts triumph over challenges. It might be thought of as a bad card because of the obstacles themselves, but the emphasis of this card is on triumph. The obstacles would be there anyway. What the card is saying is that the querent will conquer or overcome them.

Bear in mind that the conquest does not necessarily lead to a joyful conclusion with this Ace. Sometimes the triumph has a sorrowful, bittersweet quality. For a person with an incurable disease, this card could even indicate death as a triumph over suffering. Sometimes the Ace of Spades will indicate a triumph worthy of a joyful celebration, but at other times the triumph may be something for which the querent can only be solemnly grateful.

Whatever the nature of the conquest, whether the triumph is joyful or not, the Ace of Spades is almost always a positive card to see in a reading in its own way. The triumph will be something powerful and noticeable to the querent, even if the reader is unsure of how it will manifest.

Two of Spades

Contrast + Movement

The Two of Spades also hints at triumph, although not nearly as emphatically as the Ace of this suit. Like all of the other Deuces, the Two of Spades is a wild card, so you can expect the unexpected when it appears in a reading. It foretells a sudden and decisive event.

Although the coming event will be something you do not expect, there is a karmic element to this card. The card is telling you that the winds are changing, possibly in your favor but definitely in response to past or current actions. The Two of Spades embodies the Anglo-Saxon concept of *wyrd*, the unfolding of fate. It is no accident that wyrd evolved into the Modern English word *weird*, because the fates that befall us are often unexpected and can seem … well … weird.

The triumph hinted at by the Two of Spades will not necessarily lead you to what you want. The triumph here is over some imbalance in your life. It is triumphant, but it may not be what you had planned or expected. The Two of Spades is a card of destiny.

Three of Spades

Seedlings + Movement

With the Three of Spades, events are set in motion against the querent, who will find little reward in efforts expended. Whatever the querent's plan is, it simply is not going to happen, at least not in any measurable way.

The way around this is to be creative and take a different course of action than originally planned. Current actions are not going to work out. The problem can ultimately be resolved in a satisfactory way, but only if the querent has the wisdom to abandon current plans and try another tactic. The querent's current plans will result in a lot of work with very little, if any, reward.

This does not mean the querent should just give up. Whatever this problem is, it could become significantly worse if the querent does not address the issue. You have the seedlings of progress, but they must be nurtured appropriately. What the Three of Spades is saying is that the querent should not keep approaching the problem from the same angle. The querent may even need to change course more than once, much like a sailor tacking into the wind.

In a reading, if the Three of Spades falls next to a court card (a Jack, Queen, or King) of any suit, then a person fitting the description of the court card may be an ally who will help the querent find a better course of action.

Four of Spades

Stability + Movement

The Four of Spades presents the contradiction of stasis and motion. Instead of flowing freely, the energy here is blocked up, circling around and around. The end result is frustration and annoyance. Although it might be possible to turn the situation into something more productive, in order to break through the blockage, this card suggests that you might do better to ignore whatever the source of the annoyance is.

The Fours indicate stubborn situations that are resistant to change. Here, with the Four of Spades, it is change itself, it is the motion of events in your life, that is being resisted. The buildup of energy can make the situation seem larger and worse than it actually is. This is why ignoring the problem for now may be the best choice for you. This card is saying that you will be facing irritating circumstances but nothing disastrous. By feeding more energy into the situation, you could actually exacerbate the problem.

Despite the general negative tone of this card, the Four of Spades can actually be good to see in a reading. When you know that you will be confronted with aggravations, it can be easier to keep things in perspective and step away from the situation. The annoyance described by the Four of Spades is not something you can easily change, but it *is* something you can ignore.

Five of Spades

Dynamic + Movement

Dynamic motion is not always a good thing. The Five of Spades usually represents a storm in your life. It foretells unexpected obstacles and difficulties, forces pushing against you. These will result in extra work for the querent, but they are challenges that can eventually be overcome. This is where the "dynamic" part comes in. This card is good in that it usually implies ultimate achievement, but, as in any good adventure, there will be problems along the way.

The Five of Spades is similar to the Three of this suit, but more dramatic. And while the Three of Spades advises the querent to take a different, creative course of action, the Five suggests that the querent can achieve success by persevering. This card says that it is possible to achieve the goal, but there will be considerably more work involved than anticipated.

With the Five of Spades, the challenges that the querent faces may be the work of one specific person. If so, whatever this person is saying or doing, it is happening behind the querent's back; it isn't something that will be easy to confront. If the challenge is not caused by an individual, it will still be unexpected rather than anything the querent can plan for. The Five of Spades speaks of a person or event that only hinders the querent, though. With hard work, the querent will ultimately succeed.

Six of Spades

Depletion + Movement

The depletion of motion is exactly what it sounds like: the winds that once filled your sails have grown still. When the Six of Spades appears in your reading, it means the level of energy has diminished.

However, the Six of Spades may actually be a good card to see. The depletion of energy or motion is something that can be corrected. This card lets you know that you may need to invest more energy in whatever situation it is addressing. It is something you can alter by your own actions and choices.

In any event, even if you don't take steps to avoid it, the loss described by the Six of Spades will be a temporary thing. There will be some depletion of energy; the only question is how much and how long it will linger—and you have some control over those variables.

Seven of Spades

Completion + Movement

Here we have another card showing forces moving against the querent's interests, but the Sevens are cards of completion. The situation described by the Seven of Spades is not a prediction, but rather is something that is already in place. The querent is in a delicate or problematic position involving one or more other people.

That's the bad news, but it really is not "news," because it is something that the querent is currently working through. The real news is a somewhat more hopeful message indicated by this card: the problematic situation is reaching completion, so things will soon be improving for the querent. The Seven of Spades is not saying that everything will be resolved today or even tomorrow, but there will soon be a noticeable upswing for the querent. The best thing for the querent to do is to let things run their course.

An improved situation does not mean that all of the querent's wishes will be fulfilled. For example, suppose a querent has a huge crush on a classmate but doesn't know if that person feels the same way. The Seven of Spades suggests that the querent will soon learn the answer to this. The situation will then be resolved, even though the classmate might not have any interest in the querent at all. Or maybe they do. Either way, the querent will be able to move on past that awkward phase of uncertainty. Usually the resolution implied by the Seven of Spades is a positive or at least satisfactory one, but you have to be careful when interpreting this card. As with the Deuce of this suit, the end result with the Seven of Spades is often different from what the querent planned for or expected.

Eight of Spades

Manifestation + Movement

The Eight of Spades appears in a reading to tell you that motion and changes are about to come into full force. You are at a turning point where your current situation is more important than you may realize. This card is almost the opposite of the Six of Spades. Whereas the Six of this suit predicts a depletion of energy, the Eight of Spades predicts an abundance.

There is nothing symbolic or philosophical about this card. The coming changes will be overt and significant. Even if you are anticipating the event, it will be more consequential than you envisioned. This could be either good or bad, but the Eight of Spades usually implies a positive outcome. It is only a bad card if you do not want to see change, because this card predicts changes coming in a very big way. It is telling you that this is an especially significant moment in your life.

Nine of Spades

Wisdom + Movement

The Nines speak of wisdom in some way, but for the suits of Spades and Clubs, they are indicative of a lack of wisdom. With the Nine of Spades, the wisdom will come eventually, one way or another, but the querent will be happier if it is sooner rather than later. This card is a warning. When the Nine of Spades appears in a reading, it is saying that the querent needs to develop a more responsible attitude. It is important to carefully consider how your present choices and actions will affect the future.

If the querent does not examine the current situation wisely and meticulously, there will be an unpleasant outcome. The good news is that the querent has the potential to make good decisions now and avoid suffering a painful lesson later. The Nine of Spades indicates a process of change during which the querent should steer clear of foolish choices as much as possible. This does not mean they should avoid the situation. When the Nine of Spades appears, the querent needs to take responsibility, but in a careful and thoughtful way.

Ten of Spades

Force + Movement

The Ten of Spades is the force that will huff and puff and blow your dreams away. It is a force as powerful as the Ace of this suit, but instead of bringing a triumph, the Ten of Spades brings sorrow and melancholy. Whether the predicted outcome is violent or subtle, it is always sad. This is one card that never has a positive interpretation.

The sorrow expressed by the Ten of Spades might not be directed at you. If you have drawn cards to find out why a friend, relative, or romantic interest has been acting aloof and distant, this card tells you that the other party is dealing with personal issues. If the Ten of Spades falls next to the Jack of Hearts, somebody close to you will be struck with sorrow.

In numerology, the number ten reduces to one (1 + 0 = 1). The Tens are usually very solitary cards that indicate events affecting only the querent, except in the very social suit of Hearts. For the Ten of Spades, this isolation can be accompanied by an intense feeling of loneliness. The loneliness may or may not be connected to other sorrowful events described by the same card. The Ten of Spades mirrors the Ace of this suit by becoming its exact opposite. While the Ace of Spades represents conquest, the Ten of Spades is defeat.

There really is no cheery side to this card.

Jack of Spades

If you are over forty years old, the Jack of Spades represents a younger person. If you are under forty, the person could be your own age or even a few years older, but it is somebody you perceive as less experienced. Either way, this is an unhappy person, someone dissatisfied with their current situation.

The dissatisfaction will not always be readily apparent. There is often an element of deceit involved. This could even be self-deceit; the dissatisfaction could be your own. In this interpretation, the Jack of Spades is *you*, perceiving yourself as inexperienced because you feel helpless and unable to change the situation.

More often, though, the Jack of Spades represents someone else. People represented by this card may have no hostile intentions toward you, but they are not being entirely honest with you either.

Queen of Spades

The Queen of this suit can be interpreted in two different ways. The first is as a typical court card, representing a person, in this case usually a woman of some maturity. If the querent is under the age of forty, this is always an older person, but she could still be quite young. After all, a sixteen-year-old girl is "older" if the querent is only fourteen! If the querent is over the age of forty, the Queen represents a mature person who is also forty or older, even if she is somewhat younger than the querent, as long as she is someone perceived by the querent as being experienced and mature.

The Queen of Spades doesn't describe any type of personality; it only tells us that a mature person will play a significant role in the querent's life at this time.

The other interpretation of this card is unrelated to gender roles and may not even indicate a person. The Queen of Spades can sometimes indicate the burden of duty. This is not really a bad interpretation, but it does mean your plans may have to take a back seat to your obligations and responsibilities.

If you have even a trace of psychic talent, you will know which interpretation to apply when this card comes up in a reading. One interpretation will make sense and feel right, while the other will not. Trust your intuition here.

King of Spades

Like the Queen of this suit, the King of Spades has two possible interpretations, and the first is that a mature man will play a significant role in your life. How old this man might be is relative to your own age to some extent, exactly as it is with the Queen. If you are forty or older, this King is someone who is also at least forty. If you are under forty, he could be any age, but he will be older or as old as you. This man is usually someone who is steady and reliable.

The second interpretation of this card still indicates a person and, as with the Queen, is unrelated to gender. Here the King of Spades represents an enemy. This is somebody who is out to get you. It is somebody who can conceivably cause significant problems for you.

Again, you have to rely on your intuition to determine which message this card is conveying in a reading, but one of the two almost always stands out.

Seven

The Suit of Clubs

The Clubs represent the warm, dry element of Fire. In its natural state, fire is often a dangerous, devastating force, but it is also an element that we routinely harness and use. Its power is to transform. Fire changes wood, cloth, paper, and other combustibles into ash. It clears away old growth in a forest to make way for new, green saplings to arise.

In this way, Fire is similar to the element of Air in that it creates changes that can be either beneficial or destructive. But whereas Air represents movement, Fire represents transformation. The suit of Clubs speaks of personal changes more often than external events. While the things happening around you can influence your thoughts and actions, the Clubs emphasize your reactions rather than the circumstances themselves.

You have much more control over your own reactions than you do over the events around you, and in this way the Clubs are good to see in a reading. When a Club appears to present a bad omen in a reading, think of it as a warning, giving you advice to avoid potential problems as or before they arise.

In the earliest card decks, those that eventually evolved into what we now know as Tarot cards and playing cards, the Clubs were represented as polo-sticks. In Tarot decks, they retain a stick-like imagery and are often pictured as wands, staves, or rods. The Clubs in a deck of playing cards bear little resemblance to these images, but they can still wield all the power of a wizard's wand when it comes to personal transformation.

Ace of Clubs

Power + Transformation

This is your ultimate power card, a card of achievement. In a reading, the Ace of Clubs describes you as having a strong reputation and a secure place in your social unit.

That social unit can be almost anything—your family, the local government, your neighborhood, or your coven—as long as that unit is important to you.

With the force of this Ace, a transformation has already occurred within you. A part of your destiny has achieved (or will soon achieve) actualization. Returning to the image of the Club as a rod-like instrument, imagine it as a scepter held by a monarch.

In a multiple-card reading, the Ace of Clubs may be describing someone else in your life. It depends on where the card falls and what other cards are around it. Even so, the person who has come (or will come) into this power is almost always an ally of yours, so the card is still nice to see. If the Ace of Clubs bears any warning, it might be a gentle reminder of how easily you could fall from a high pedestal. Overall, though, this Ace brings a positive message.

Two of Clubs

Contrast + Transformation

When this wild card appears in a reading, the querent can expect some emotional release. The Deuces always indicate that the querent should be prepared for surprising events, but with the Two of Clubs, those events are likely to elicit a deeply emotional response. On a superficial level, this may seem more appropriate for the suit of Hearts, but the Two of Clubs does not generate emotion; it transforms emotion.

If you have drawn the Two of Clubs as a solitary card, it simply indicates that something unexpected is going to happen. When the Two of Clubs comes up in a reading with multiple cards, however, it is usually influencing one or more cards that fall adjacent to it. If it falls next to the Six of Diamonds, the querent may lose some money due to unexpected events. Next to the Four of Hearts it suggests that the querent is going to be surprised by one or more friends.

Three of Clubs
Seedlings + Transformation

The Clubs are all about personal transformation, about your reactions to the events unfolding around you. When you see the Three of Clubs in a reading, it means you are resisting this transformation. The potential for transformation has very little force behind it. It is only a seedling, and it will perish without some care. Change, transformation, is essential to a healthy life. It occurs naturally unless there is some resistance. The Three of Clubs tells you that there is a problem, and you are the one creating it.

Most likely you are not even aware of this. You think everything you are doing is just fine, but it is not. You need to look at what you are doing and make some changes. Apologies may even be in order.

It is very easy to think you are doing the right thing when really you are just repeating comfortable patterns of behavior. The Three of Clubs tells you that it is time to make some changes in those behaviors.

Four of Clubs
Stability + Transformation

The fires are still small and tentative when this card comes up. Here you are not resisting transformation, as with the Three of this suit, but you are not fully participating in it either. The Four of Clubs is saying that you are oblivious to what is going on around you. For some reason, you are blind to the situation.

It is difficult, of course, to move forward when you cannot see your way clearly. This card is not suggesting you do anything rash; it is simply saying that you are not making smart choices. Now might be a good time to step back and reassess what you are doing, who you can trust, and where you are investing your time and energy. The Four of Clubs is not an especially bad card to see in a reading, but it is not great either. There is something that you just are not noticing, and the situation is not going to change until you wake up and see it.

Five of Clubs

Dynamic + Transformation

This is the adventure you do not want to have. It can change you and it will certainly be interesting, but the Five of Clubs is a warning not to touch the fire. It is something best avoided. Otherwise, you will almost surely get burned.

When the Five of Clubs appears, it is telling the querent to give up and move on. The problem is that this particular situation in your life is wild, dynamic, and out of control. Even if you are successful in your pursuit, the end result will be unsatisfying. Yes, there will be transformation, but it will be more than expected and not at all what you wanted. The card indicates a lost cause that will only lead to disappointment if the querent continues to pursue it. There is usually some illusion of control here, but it is no more than an illusion. Some fires cannot be controlled. The querent might be able to avoid breaking up with their boyfriend, but afterward the relationship still won't be any good. It will transform into something unpleasant. Like the Rolling Stones told us, you can't always get what you want. When we are aware of this, it can be easier to cut bait and direct our efforts elsewhere.

Six of Clubs

Depletion + Transformation

The Six of Clubs is one of the more abstract cards. The transformative fires are depleted, but what does that mean?

For one thing, it can indicate frustration. The Six of Clubs often indicates a conflict that you are angry about but that you cannot (or don't feel you can) attack directly. Instead, you internalize that anger. It is a slow, smoldering anger that can affect you deeply, even physically.

Which brings us to another possible interpretation: sometimes the Six of Clubs does indicate an actual physical imbalance. Life itself is a process of constant transformation, so illness can often be described as a depletion of that fire or energy. The person suffering may not be you. For example, in the twelve-card layout described in the next chapter, if the Six of Clubs falls in the seventh position, it means your spouse or business partner could soon become sick. No matter who the card indicates, though, the illness can often be averted if steps are taken immediately. Take a vacation day and rest up to rekindle that transformative fire.

Seven of Clubs

Completion + Transformation

The union of completion and transformation sounds like a good thing, but what this points to is better expressed as a "complete mess." This is a card of conflict, similar to the Six of this suit, but when the Seven of Clubs appears, there is nothing subtle going on. Instead of a smoldering anger, the querent faces a full firestorm. The fire is complete; it is an inferno.

You should be prepared to face some arguments and conflicts if you see the Seven of Clubs in a reading. The conflicts may be unexpected, but they are the result of issues that have been building for a while now. This is never a solo experience; other people are involved. The suit of Clubs draws our attention to personal transformation, so it is likely that some or all of the fighting going on is your own fault to some degree.

It is possible for you (or the querent) to turn this situation around, especially if the conflict has not yet erupted, but it won't be easy. The Sevens are cards of completion, so you will also need to completely change your personal behaviors. In a situation like this, a carefully constructed spell could help too (see chapter 11).

Eight of Clubs

Manifestation + Transformation

In this suit, the Eight brings money and material posses-
sions into the arena of transformation. The Eight of Clubs
often addresses your finances more directly than the
Eight of Diamonds does. While the latter can indicate fortune in any tangible or intangible form, the Eight of Clubs
focuses on material wealth.

The Eight of this suit is neither good nor bad; it can
go either way. It is possible that the transformation could
work in your favor, but very often this card is a warning.
When you see the Eight of Clubs, it will be very easy to
lose money either by investing unwisely or simply by
spending foolishly. Look for potential opportunities,
but don't take unnecessary risks and be careful not to
spend money on things you don't really need. This might
sound like it is good advice at any time, but it is especially
important when the Eight of Clubs appears in a reading.

In regard to your material resources, this card is very
similar to the Eight of Diamonds. But while the Eight of

Diamonds suggests that you cautiously move forward, the Eight of Clubs warns you to rein things in a little.

Nine of Clubs

Wisdom + Transformation

The Nines indicate a lack of wisdom in the suits of Spades and Clubs, but for the Clubs, this is not always a bad omen. Like the Eight of Clubs, the Nine of this suit can go either way. When the Nine of Clubs appears in a reading, it means that events are going to unfold in ways that the querent is not expecting. The end result could be either good or bad, or it could fall in some gray area in between, but it will certainly be a surprise. Things are not going to work out the way you have imagined, which can actually be a good thing if you are expecting something dreadful to happen.

The unexpected events are at least partially the result of your own actions and decisions. Nevertheless, the surprise element may leave you feeling helpless. The Nines describe evolving situations, though, so you may be able to step in and turn things around if the surprise turns out to be an unpleasant one. With the Nine of Clubs, you should avoid acting impulsively. It is better to wait and see where the surprising event(s) will lead before taking any action.

When the Nine of Clubs appears, it is telling you to "wait and see." In this way, it is similar to the Three of Diamonds, but this card holds the promise of a surprising and most likely pleasing and unexpected development.

Ten of Clubs

Force + Transformation

The Ten of Clubs is similar to the Ace of this suit in that it is a card of achievement. The transformation has occurred in full force and you have reached, or will soon reach, your goals. In whatever way you define success, it is coming your way.

The success described by the Ten of Clubs, however, will be a cold success. That may not be a bad thing, but it is something you should be aware of. If all that matters is whether you "win," then it is a good card to see. However, most situations and events we encounter have more layers than this. If the Ten of Clubs comes up in reference to a romantic relationship, it means you will be in control of the relationship, but what kind of romance is that? Healthy interpersonal relationships involve a give-and-take. You may be in control, but you won't be very happy. You do not want that kind of relationship with your friends either.

Like the Ten of Spades, the Ten of Clubs has a lonely, isolated quality. This can be a good card when it is speaking of pure business arrangements or of success in any competitive endeavor, because those are times when you want as much control as possible. The Ten of Clubs predicts a cold and perhaps lonely success, but sometimes victory is its own reward.

Jack of Clubs

With the suit of Clubs, the court cards represent people at different stages of personal transformation. As you might expect, the Jack of Clubs is a person in the "before" stage, but it is someone who very much wants to move forward. This person is ambitious and may even be perceived as aggressive and annoying, but they are not necessarily hostile toward the querent in any way.

Because this is a less experienced person, the Jack of Clubs is often someone younger than the querent. This is almost always the case if the querent is forty or older. For younger querents, the Jack of Clubs could be someone the same age or even older, but they will be subordinate to the querent in some way. Nevertheless, this person is also someone who can affect or influence the querent in some way, so it is a good idea to keep an eye out for an ambitious person whose goals could either help or harm the querent.

Queen of Clubs

The Queen of Clubs usually represents a woman who is older or at least more experienced than the querent. This is a woman who has found her place in life. This is a very maternal card, whether or not it indicates your biological mother. It could be your boss, a neighbor, or an older friend, or almost any person in your life if she brings a maternal quality to your relationship. The Queen of Clubs can even represent a spouse, but if so, the focus is on her as a caregiver rather than as a sexual partner.

Because of the maternal nature of this card, the Queen of Clubs can also bring a more symbolic meaning to the reading by indicating familial ties and obligations. It can sometimes refer to your family or even to your own childhood, but even here there will almost always be an older, sympathetic and supportive person involved. The Queen of Clubs might be your mother, your grandmother, an aunt, or an older sister or cousin. It could also be a male relative who plays a nurturing role in your life.

The Queen of Clubs only draws your attention to this person. It does not say whether she is helping you move forward or holding you back. That is better determined by your question and by the cards that fall next to this Queen. Even in its most negative manifestation, though, the Queen of Clubs is not hostile toward you. If she is holding you back, it is because she needs you at this time. This Queen is a sympathetic figure in your life.

King of Clubs

The King of Clubs is the masculine version of the Queen of this suit; he is an experienced, knowledgeable, and generally strong person. This is not a particularly romantic card. It's possible that the querent has a physical relationship with this person, but if so, that is not the aspect of the relationship that the King of Clubs is emphasizing. This person is well established and conservative, but not in the sense in which the latter word is used in US politics. He could be extremely progressive politically if that is the status quo in the querent's social circles. The King of Clubs is the epitome of stability and tradition.

The person indicated by this card has the potential to be an ally for the querent. Like the Queen of this suit, the King of Clubs could either benefit or obstruct the querent, but as a rule, his experience and social position are valuable resources. Like the King of Hearts, the King of Clubs usually has an approachable, easygoing personality.

Eight

Laying Out the Cards

Once you have a general idea of what the cards symbolize, you will need to observe them in some kind of context to derive meaning from them. There are different ways you can lay out the cards, with varying levels of complexity. Although you should familiarize yourself with the cards, you do not need to memorize the meaning of each and every one before trying a few readings. The best way to learn how to read cards is to begin working with them and letting them speak to you.

How Cartomancy Works

Whether we are talking about divination or more active practices like spellcasting, all magic has its own framework of internal logic. The details within this framework often vary from one culture to another, but those same details share similar principles that our subconscious minds respond to. One of these principles, and a primary concept in respect to *sortilege* (divination by drawing lots), is synchronicity. This principle acknowledges connections between simultaneous events that have no determinable correlation with each other. In both magic and divination, synchronicity is attributed to the idea that all things are connected.

Synchronicity comes into play in many modes of divination, not only in all varieties of sortilege but also in divination by observing the movements of birds and animals (*theriomancy*) or through the science of astrology. I have heard people dismiss theriomancy by saying that animals are just living out their lives, that they are not intentionally revealing omens, as if anyone seriously believes that animals and birds are scrambling around to deliver symbolic, coded messages to us. No, theriomancy works because each animal and bird is a part of our ever-unfolding universe. Each animal and bird is a part of the great universal pattern of becoming, and the task of the theriomancer is to discern shifts in that pattern by observing the movements and behaviors of various creatures.

Likewise, people who understand nothing about astrology will denounce it because, they say, stars cannot influence our lives. But real astrologers make no claims at all concerning stars. The signs of the zodiac are named for twelve constellations; they are not the constellations themselves. The zodiac consists of twelve equal sectors of the sky, each precisely thirty degrees in the 360-degree celestial circle that surrounds our world. Astrologers simply observe the patterns of the planets as they move through these sectors. (And before anyone tries to say that the Sun and Moon are not planets, let me point out that astrology uses the *original* meaning of "planet" to designate a heavenly body that appears to change its position in the sky.) This is where the cynic will point out that the gravitational fields of planets like Venus and Jupiter are far too weak to have any influence on us, which again reveals an ignorance of the principles behind astrology. Gravitational fields are irrelevant. The visible planets, like everything else, are part of the unfolding universe. They are part of the divine pattern that we are all connected to. Just as the theriomancer observes the movements of animals and birds, the astrologer observes the movements of the planets.

When you are practicing cartomancy, the cards that you draw at random are also part of the great pattern of the universe. Of course, just as the zodiac gives meaning to the movements of the planets, you will need to provide some context for the cards that you draw. This context can be achieved by drawing a single card while asking what kind of day you will have, but most of your readings will probably be more complex than this. You might do a three-card reading or even a twelve-card reading. In this chapter we will look at several ways you can lay out cards, but synchronicity is an underlying principle regardless of how you choose to draw and place the cards.

Good readers do not rely on synchronicity alone, however. Really good readers also rely on their intuition. Every language is limited in terms of what ideas it can convey through its vocabulary, and playing cards have a vocabulary of only fifty-two "words." However, the nice thing about playing cards is that their imagery is abstract, and thus the cards, the fifty-two words in the deck, are far more open to interpretation. Let the cards speak to you. This can be difficult at first when you are trying to associate each card with a general interpretation, but it gets easier as you become more familiar with your deck. If a particular card seems to mean something other than what I have said or what its numerological and elemental correspondences would suggest, go with your instinct.

The cards may also take on variant meanings to better reflect your age and environment. I have described the Five of Spades as foretelling unexpected obstacles and difficulties, but perhaps that is not the message you sense when this card comes up in your readings. If you are consistently seeing different meanings from this or any other card, do not be afraid of interpreting it as your intuition leads you to do. Trust your instincts.

You cannot connect with the cards on an intuitive level if you refer to this book every time you do a reading. After you have a general working knowledge of the cards and their interpretations, put down the book and let the cards speak to you. Otherwise, you are not reading cards; you are reading a book. You may, of course, refer to the book if you genuinely cannot remember the meaning of a card and your intuition is not filling in the blank. Use the book as you would use training wheels when first learning how to ride a bicycle. While it can be helpful at first, you do not want to continually rely on it.

A variant meaning can also come up as a one-time thing. For example, maybe the Five of Spades usually indicates unexpected obstacles, but during one of your readings you look at the card and have a strong impression that something fun and exciting will soon be happening. This is something you would expect to see expressed in Diamonds or Hearts, but perhaps this time it is exactly what the Five of Spades is trying to tell you. Trust your sixth sense when reading the cards.

You may also have a personal card that represents yourself, as I described in chapter 3. In my opinion, the personal card most often indicates yourself only when you are the querent. When you are reading for another person, that card will have its ordinary meaning. However, that is just my opinion, and you may ignore it if your intuition is screaming that the personal card represents yourself, regardless of who you are reading for.

While it is important to listen to your sixth sense, it is equally important not to allow your imagination to run wild. You may want to keep a journal of your readings. Watch for personal bias. If most of your readings involve meeting a tall, dark stranger, then you are probably letting your personal desires interfere with true seership—unless, of course, you discover that you actually are meeting a lot of tall, dark strangers! The journal does not have to be anything fancy; something as simple as a spiral notebook will work just fine. Once you are comfortable trusting your intuition, you can dispense with the journal if you wish, but it can be an extremely helpful tool when you are first learning to read cards.

One way to keep your imagination in check is to focus your mind before you begin the reading. This can be accomplished through a short meditation or simply by concentrating on your breathing for a minute or two. Inhale to the count of four, hold the breath for an equal count, then release your breath slowly to a final count of four. Repeat this until you feel a sense of relaxation flow through you.

Alternatively, some readers like to prepare themselves through prayer. There is no one way to do this, but the prayer should, of course, reflect your own spirituality. A reader who believes that the universe is governed by one single deity will obviously pray to that deity for guidance. If you follow a polytheistic path, however, you may want to direct your prayer to a deity specifically related to prophecy or magic. Some appropriate choices include the following:

Spiritual Culture	Deity(ies)
Hellenic/Greek	Apollo, Hecate
Egyptian	Isis, Thoth
Roman	Apollo
Briton	Sulis
Welsh	Bran the Blessed
Anglo-Saxon	Woden
Scandinavian	Odin, Mímir

These are just suggestions, of course. The deity to whom you direct your prayer should be, above all else, one with whom you already have an established relationship. In other words, if you follow the Hellenic pantheon and often give offerings to Hera, then it is entirely appropriate for you to pray to Hera for guidance even if she is not usually associated with divination. The gods, after all, are not one-dimensional. Your connection with a deity is more important than the aspects of life that the deity is traditionally associated with.

Speaking of offerings, some readers like to give something to the deity prior to or while requesting guidance.

This can be a libation of wine or mead or some incense burned in a censer. If the offering would distract you from the work at hand, you can give it later, but it is a good idea to give something in gratitude to a deity when asking for guidance.

Readers who do include prayer may want to reserve it for more important readings. If you are drawing a card every morning to see what the day might bring, there probably is no need for a formal prayer. And when you do pray, if you do, it need not be a lengthy soliloquy. Your prayer can be as simple as "(Name of deity), I ask for your guidance."

The very act of shuffling the deck can also help prepare you for the reading. While shuffling, put aside any extraneous thoughts going through your mind. If you find that you are better prepared when you concentrate on your breathing, this can be done while you shuffle the cards. When shuffling, you are doing more than just randomizing the cards in the deck. You are preparing yourself as well, so continue shuffling for as long as you feel you need to. At a certain point you will feel centered and ready, and this is when you should set the deck down. If reading for yourself, you can now draw your cards. When reading for someone else, invite the querent to shuffle the deck now. This will help the querent to mentally prepare for the reading, and, due to another magical principle known as the law of contagion, the shuffling will connect the querent with the cards before you begin. The law of contagion states that any two things that come into contact remain connected after they are separated. Contagion is why spellcasters may want an article of clothing or a similar personal item belonging to the person they are working magic for. In cinema, this is usually depicted as nefarious magic, but the principle is just as valuable when working any kind of beneficial spell. Using this same principle, you are allowing the querent to connect with the cards through the act of shuffling.

Just as you did before passing your cards to the querent, the other person should continue shuffling the deck for as long as needed. Do not try to assess whether the querent has shuffled long enough. Some querents will sense the process of contagion as they shuffle and will put the cards down after only two or three shuffles. This is fine. The important thing is that they feel comfortable with the deck, not that they have handled the cards for any specific length of time. Conversely, you will occasionally have a querent who continues shuffling the deck far longer than you think is necessary. This is fine also. It is not your place to decide when your querent is sufficiently comfortable with the cards for the reading to begin.

After the deck has been shuffled sufficiently, have the querent cut it into three equal parts using their left hand. Have them pick up the top part of the deck with their left hand and place that pile on the table. Then have them take another part of the original pile and place it on the table. Do this personally if you are reading for yourself. Watch and remember which part of the deck was on the top, the middle, and the bottom.

Then, also using your left hand, reassemble the deck by putting the middle part on the top part and both of these on the bottom part.

This final step is purely symbolic. The deck is cut into three parts because three is the number of creativity and expression. You are symbolically asking the cards to express the pattern of the unfolding universe, to reveal the web of wyrd. And the left hand is used (by both you and the querent if this is someone other than yourself) because it is symbolically the receptive, psychic hand. Cutting and reassembling the deck is a nice transition between preparing yourself and actually drawing the cards.

Choosing a Type of Reading

When you draw cards from the top of the deck, you need to peruse them in some context. As I mentioned earlier, this can be as simple as drawing a single card as you mentally ask yourself, "What kind of day will I (or the querent) have today?" In fact, this is a good exercise to help you develop a relationship with your cards.

The One-Card Reading

The one-card reading is useful when you want a quick, concise answer. The context can be almost any question you choose as long as it can be answered with a yes or a no. Should you go out to that party where you won't know many of the other guests? Is this a good day to begin a new sewing project? Will you have a good day at school or the office? One-card readings do not give literal yes or no answers, but the questions posed should be simple and straightforward, because a single card is not going to give a complex, detailed response.

Usually you will want an answer with more depth when consulting the cards, and for that you will draw a number of cards to provide the necessary context in your reading.

The Three-Card Layout

This easy layout is a step above the single card reading, but the type of question it answers is still the same.

Draw one card and lay it out in front of you. This is the primary response. Consider the meaning associated with the card and then draw two more, placing one card to the left of the primary card and the other to the right. These secondary cards modify or clarify the primary card.

As an example, you could ask, "Should I go to that party even though I will not know many of the other guests?" This provides a context for the information that your three cards will give.

You draw your primary card and see that it is the King of Diamonds. This card indicates a mature man who is harboring some secret.

The next card you draw is the Nine of Spades, so you put that to the left of the King of Diamonds. The Nine of Spades indicates a lack of wisdom on your part; it's a warning that you could easily do something foolish.

The third card, placed to the right of the King of Diamonds, is the King of Hearts. This represents a mature, experienced male, but it is not indicating another man; the secondary cards modify and clarify the first card you drew in this layout. Here the King of Hearts is revealing that the man mentioned in this reading is benign and probably someone you already have a relationship of some kind with. If you are sexually attracted to men, this reading could indicate a budding romantic relationship. If not, or if you are not in the market for such a relationship, the man is most likely someone who is or will become a good friend.

Interpreting these three cards, you can expect to meet up with a man at the party who has some kind of surprise or secret that you may not be immediately aware of. There is nothing bad about the secret, but it could lead you to do something foolish. You can go to the party and have fun, but refrain from making any promises, agreements, or commitments.

The Past-Present-Future Layout

This layout also uses three cards, but you do not ask a specific question. Instead, the context is derived from the order in which the cards are drawn and the positions you place them in. This allows the cards to speak to you more freely than if you ask a specific question.

Draw your first card from the top of the deck and place it before you. This card represents the past. It is where you are coming from.

Now draw a second card and place it to the right of the first one. The second card represents the present. It is what you are going through now. In this reading, the concept of "now" can be a little subjective. The card can be addressing something you have already almost completely experienced, or it can be something that is only now just beginning. The card describes something touching you in the present, however, rather than something completely in the past or future.

Finally, draw a third card and place it to the right of the other two. The third card, of course, represents the future. It is where you are heading. It is not necessarily where you will arrive; it is where your path is most likely to lead. This layout is also sometimes called "from-through-to." It describes where you are coming from, what you are going through, and where this is all likely to lead you to.

As an example, let's say we draw the following three cards:

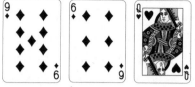

In the first position we have the Nine of Diamonds. This card is *wisdom + fortune* and typically means that the querent's finances and reputation are protected. Since this card is in the past position, it indicates that the querent has been in a reasonably comfortable position. It describes where the querent is coming from.

In the second position is the Six of Diamonds. *Depletion + fortune* tells us that the querent is going through a minor financial crisis or is about to do so. Because of the past, because of where the querent is coming from, we can surmise that this financial challenge is not anything disastrous. A different card in the past position, perhaps the Three of Diamonds or the Eight of Clubs, would tell a very different story. A different card could even demand a different interpretation of the present position. In this reading, we see a loss of money, something for the querent to be aware of but probably not overly concerned about.

In the third position is the Queen of Hearts. From the present situation (loss of money), the querent will be moving toward an experienced woman. But what does that mean? Perhaps she is a future mentor or a lover. Divination is not an exact science, but this third card is unusually vague, seemingly unrelated to the other two. When this occurs in your past-present-future reading, you may draw a clarification card.

Clarification Cards

In the basic three-card layout, there are already two cards that clarify or modify the primary card. In the past-present-future layout and the five-card layout (which we will look at next), you may occasionally need a little help in understanding what a card is trying to say. You should never draw more than one card for this, and then only if you are really having some difficulty understanding one of the cards you have already drawn, not just because you dislike or disagree with the outcome.

In the example just given for the past-present-future layout, the cards in the past and present positions clarify each other fairly well. But then we have the Queen of Hearts in the future position, and that does not make a lot of sense. Who is this Queen, what is her relationship with the querent, and why would anyone care? To get a better idea of what the card might be saying, we can draw one clarification card.

We do this, drawing the Ten of Hearts and placing it just over the Queen of Hearts. The Ten of Hearts is *force + emotion*. This emotion is very often romantic in nature, reminding us that sometimes the Queen of Hearts conveys the more abstract concept of passion. Now we can see what the Queen is saying. The querent will be going through a financial loss, but those circumstances will ultimately lead to an exciting romance, perhaps not a "happily ever after," but assuredly something wonderful and stimulating.

Let me emphasize that a clarification card should be drawn only when necessary. If a card does not make sense from the perspective of numerology and its elemental association but you have an intuitive understanding of what it is trying to say, that in itself is sufficient and no clarification card is needed.

The Five-Card Layout

The five-card layout is similar to the past-present-future layout, but it includes two extra cards representing people, situations, or conditions that are either moving you forward or holding you back.

Place card 4 above the present card. This card represents something that is or will be moving you forward. It often indicates assistance of some kind, but not always. Conflicts, enemies, and crises are all very non-helpful things that nevertheless drive us onward.

Place card 5 below the present card to see what is or will be holding you back. Just as the fourth card is not always a feel-good, positive influence, this fifth card is not necessarily something you perceive as bad. If you are in a toxic relationship and the Ace of Hearts is your fifth card in the reading, it is your love for the other person that is holding you back from what you need to do. In the same situation, the Four of Diamonds would indicate that it is your stability, or rather your fear of losing stability, that is holding you back.

The five-card layout is my favorite for most purposes. It gives me an idea of what is going on, and additionally tells me what to look for and what to avoid.

The Twelve-Card Layout

The twelve-card layout can be a more difficult layout to master because of the number of cards, but it is also one of my favorites because of the same complexity found in the five-card layout. As with the past-present-future layout, the context of the reading comes from where the cards fall, so there is no need to pose a question. You certainly can ask a question with this reading, but the cards are more likely to tell you what you *need* to know rather than what you *want* to know. Each of the twelve positions represents one facet of your life.

After the deck has been shuffled and cut, draw twelve cards from the top and lay them in front of you in this order:

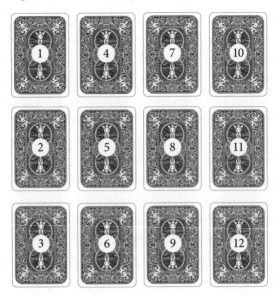

Card 1 represents either yourself or the querent (when reading for another person).

Card 2 says something about your resources, what you have to work with. This can be your money, your influence, your experience, your savings. Sometimes this card can refer to your inner resources. It could speak of your will-power or spirituality or even your general health.

Card 3 is people outside your immediate family whom you have an extended connection with. This includes neighbors and fairly close relatives such as aunts, uncles, and cousins. If you have any neo-tribal relationships, such as a coven or a kindred, the card falling here may be speaking of your fellow members in that collective. Here you will find the influences that ground and center you.

Card 4 is your past. It can be the distant past, as far back as your childhood. If you have moved to another city since then, it can refer to your hometown. In practical terms, the card that falls here reveals past influences that are affecting you now.

Card 5 is your creativity card. It is concerned with your creative expression. If you have any creative hobbies, such as writing or art or music, this card may have something to say about them. It can also foretell upcoming social interactions, but specifically how those interactions will stimulate or otherwise affect your own creativity. It can even include fleeting romantic encounters. Creativity emerges from some sort of passion, which can vary from one person to another. The card that falls here is speaking about those activities and events that inspire you and drive you forward.

Card 6 describes your duties, your unavoidable responsibilities. This often has to do with your job, but it can refer to any obligation. As with the card in position 2, the card that falls here can also be saying something about your health, since personal health is something we all have a duty to maintain as well as we can.

Card 7 concerns your partner. If you are married, this very likely means your spouse, but it can be anyone you share an equal partnership with. It could be a business or investment partner. This card will sometimes speak of a very close friend, someone close enough to be considered a social partner but on a platonic level.

Card 8 represents your partner's resources. It has the same meaning in relationship to your partner as card 2 does in relationship to you. This is your partner's money and influence; it is what they can bring to the table.

Card 9 has to do with travel, although not necessarily in the physical sense. This card could have something to do with a physical journey, but it more often describes some kind of mental or spiritual growth.

Card 10 is your future. It is your ambition and where you are going, or at least where you hope to be going. This card describes your goals, the opportunities you will have, or the hurdles you must overcome.

Card 11 reflects the people and situations affected by your creative expression, and in this way it often interacts with card 5. If you play a musical instrument, this card could predict a paying gig or even a recording contract. It speaks of other people and how they respond to you. This card could even foretell a lasting relationship developing in the wake of a romantic encounter. Very often the card reveals events concerning friends, in particular friends who are drawn to your own creative style. These are usually not people you have just met; they are people you have known for a while. If it is someone you recently met or will soon meet, this is someone you will have a long-term relationship with in some way.

Card 12 speaks of your subconscious. It often reveals something that is holding you back and that you are not aware of. This is a card of secrets and deception, whether someone else is doing the deceiving or it is a trick of your own mind.

You may have already noticed pairings in this layout where one card may clarify or even modify another, such as cards 3 (grounding) and 9 (expansion), cards 4 (past) and 10 (future), and cards 5 (romantic encounters) and 11 (lasting relationships). In each of these pairings, the two cards are six spaces apart. If you were to arrange the twelve cards in a circle, like the numbers on a clock, you would see that these pairings are opposite each other. You may even prefer to lay the cards out in a circular pattern. However you place them, when you interpret a card, be sure to look at the card it is paired with to see if that contributes anything to its meaning.

Your intuitive faculty might also detect other patterns in the cards. During a reading you may see that the guy you have been flirting with (card 5) at your office or other workplace (card 6) is hiding something from you (card 12), even though none of this fits with the pairings that I have described. Any card in the layout might be connected with any other card, so you really need to use your intuition. This is where a journal comes in handy when you are first learning to read playing cards. Writing down what you see in the reading can help clarify the message.

With the twelve-card layout, the cards can also speak to you individually on an intuitive level. As you look at a card, pay attention to the feeling you get from it. In general, there are four different responses you may have when you look at a specific card:

1. **The card jumps out and screams at you.** This may be your reaction to one or two cards in the reading, and of course if this happens then those are the cards you need to pay the most attention to. Very often the other cards in the layout are little more than modifiers for the principal message.

2. **The card seems significant in the reading, but its meaning doesn't really make sense to you.** When this happens, if you still don't understand the card after drawing all twelve and looking at all possible patterns, draw another card for clarification and place it on the one you don't understand. The second card should give you a better idea of what the first is trying to convey. It is rare to need more than a single clarification card. If more than three cards in the reading require clarification, put the deck away for a day or so and try again later.

3. **The card doesn't have any meaning at all for you.** This is different from not understanding the meaning of a card or (particularly if you are new to cartomancy) not remembering what the card usually indicates. You look at the card and there is just nothing there. This is okay. Sometimes a card will only be a placeholder, an empty space where nothing needs to be said. There shouldn't be more than one or two of these at the most in a reading, however. If more than three cards have this sense of nothingness, put the deck away and try again later. Divination is not something that can be forced.

4. **You have no special reaction to the card.** The meaning of the card is more or less what you would expect it to be when taking into consideration its position in the reading and the other cards that fall around it. This is how you will, or should, react to most of the cards that you draw.

Note that these are *intuitive* reactions to the cards. You may also have your own unique interpretations for several cards in your deck for other reasons, such as a personal card derived from numerology and your zodiac sign (as I described in chapter 3).

As an example of a twelve-card reading, try to envision the following cards laid out in the prescribed pattern.

If it helps, you can even pick these cards out of a deck and place them in front of you.

The first card is the King of Diamonds, setting the tone for the reading by revealing that you have some kind of hidden agenda. Glancing immediately to the twelfth card (Ten of Clubs), we see the achievement and cold control within your own subconscious, so you are well aware of what you are hiding. The Kings usually represent males, but in this layout, having the King of Diamonds in the first position supersedes this. It represents you, regardless of your gender.

The second card, representing your resources, is the King of Hearts. If you are a man, the card could represent you and your own experience, but it more likely represents an ally or an older mentor, regardless of your gender. The cards are telling you to watch for this mentor who can help you achieve your hidden goal.

A problem is seen when you look at the third card drawn, the Six of Clubs. This indicates frustration and stagnant energy and is connected to a person or persons close to you. We can see that it is paired with the Ten of Spades in the ninth position (because the two cards are six positions apart), suggesting that you will experience sorrow and sadness if things don't change. Looking at the other cards in the layout doesn't shed any more light on this, so let's draw a clarification card and lay it on the Six of Clubs. Your clarification card is the Five of Clubs, the card of lost causes. There is a toxic relationship somewhere in your life that you need to step away from to avoid that Ten of Spades in the ninth position. This is tied in somehow with your hidden agenda with whatever it is that you don't want others to see.

The fourth card drawn, the Three of Hearts, encourages you to recall a hobby or a simple activity from your past. This card is paired with the Ace of Diamonds in the tenth position. The Ace of Diamonds is one of the most fortunate cards in the deck, and in this reading it represents your future. These cards seem to be saying that the problems you are experiencing now will not have a lasting impact on your life.

The fifth card is the Six of Diamonds, indicating a loss of money. There's not much you can do about this, and it doesn't seem significant in the reading since the Nine of Diamonds is protecting your financial situation in the following (sixth) position. These cards may indicate that you have recently lost someone or soon will, but your overall financial position is stable.

The seventh and eighth cards, representing your partner (Queen of Hearts) and your partner's resources (Ten of Hearts), are very encouraging in this reading. Interpreting what kind of partner the cards are referencing depends on whether you are male or female and whether you are attracted to men or women or both. In any configuration, we see a deeply emotional relationship with someone who can be a great source of strength and support at this time.

With the eleventh card (Seven of Clubs), you are warned about a fight or conflict with one of your friends. This ties in with the Six of Clubs and the Ten of Spades.

Finally, the Ten of Clubs as your twelfth card tells us that you are very well aware of your secret and are ultimately in control of the situation.

Notice how the twelve-card layout gives a much more detailed reading. The trick is in identifying where the primary message is. In this case, it involves a person with whom the querent should sever ties. The remaining cards expand on this to remind the querent to guard a personal secret and to be assured that this problem is finite and will not affect the querent's life in the long run.

Sample Readings

You have read about how to lay out and interpret the cards. To illustrate how this works, I gave readings to a few people using several different layouts.

A Past-Present-Future Reading

Allie Schumacher is a professional Tarot reader. Like every good reader (whether using playing cards or a Tarot deck), she knows the value of receiving a reading from somebody else. It is difficult to be entirely impartial when reading for yourself, so a reading from someone else can offer some perspective that you did not have before.

For Allie's reading, I drew three cards, laying them out from left to right. The first card, representing Allie's past, was the Ten of Clubs. This card is all about being in control. At first it confused Allie, because she did not feel like she was in control of her life at all. But the card directed her to examine her past, where she was coming from, more closely. She was the mother of two beautiful children, independent, and working professionally as a Tarot reader. While everything in her life was not perfect, she had assumed much more control than she realized.

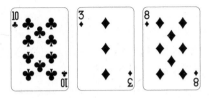

The second card was the Three of Diamonds, a card that says "not yet." This was Allie's present. The card told me that she was still striving for more in her life. For Allie, it was a reminder that life is a journey, not a goal.

Then for the third card I drew the Eight of Diamonds. The Eights are cards of manifestation, and this one was describing Allie's future. It connected with the Three of Diamonds, changing the statement from "not yet" to "not yet, but soon." The Eight of Diamonds was a reassurance that Allie's life was moving forward. She is in control, and has been for some time, and will attain her goals if she keeps going as she is now.

Another Past-Present-Future Reading

It takes some courage to read cards because what you see is not always going to be rainbows and lollipops.

Wynn Willow is an attractive young witch with a loving husband and three wonderful children. She wanted a simple, general reading about her health. Wynn has received many blessings, and this was reflected when I placed the Eight of Hearts in the position representing her past.

Then, to look at her present, I drew the Six of Clubs. This card very often indicates illness. Its presence in the reading did not surprise either of us. This was why she wanted a reading.

When I drew a third card to look at her future, I pulled the Three of Spades. This card indicates that Wynn has a lot of work to do, and will see very little reward for her effort. Like the previous card, this was not entirely surprising.

Wynn had recently been diagnosed with lupus, an autoimmune disease for which there is no known cure. The cards had nothing good to say about this. This is why divination should never be approached like a parlor game. Sometimes we are confronted with harsh and difficult challenges, and the cards can reflect this.

That does not mean that a "dark" reading such as this one has no value. Wynn is a strong woman, and she will face this disease with fortitude and resolve. Knowing that her efforts will see only a little reward can shield her from future disappointment. When we are aware of the challenges ahead, we are better prepared to meet them.

A Five-Card Reading

Chris Robertson was looking for some guidance concerning his domestic life. I decided to try a five-card layout, since this gives indications of what drives us forward and what holds us back.

Remember that the five-card layout is essentially a past-present-future reading with the addition of two extra cards. I began by drawing a card representing his past, and this was the Six of Hearts. This card is emotional depletion, often manifesting as arguments and conflicts of interest.

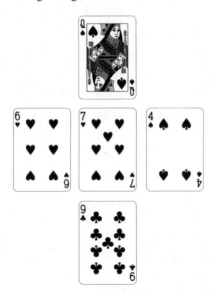

The second card I drew, for Chris's present, was the marriage card itself, the Seven of Hearts. This told me that we were looking not just at his domestic life in general, but specifically at his marriage.

For his future, I pulled the Four of Spades, a card of blocked energy. The Four of Spades speaks of frustration and annoyances. By this time, it was clear to me that we were looking at divorce, and this was verified when I drew the Queen of Spades as the card showing what was moving him forward. The Queens almost always represent women, and the Queen of Spades hints at some kind of duty, like maybe the duty one has to a spouse.

Chris was surprised by the accuracy of this reading. He and his wife had recently agreed to divorce, recognizing that neither of them was happy and fulfilled in the relationship. The only thing that surprised him was the Four of Spades, as he was anticipating an amicable parting. But the process of divorce is often fraught with frustration and annoyances. Knowing this in advance will help prepare Chris for the experience.

The cards had one more piece of advice for him. The fifth card, showing what could hold him back, was the Nine of Clubs. This card warned him to avoid acting impulsively. The Nine of Clubs tells us to approach things with caution. This is always good advice when facing a divorce, especially if it is a friendly divorce. No matter how amicable the two parties are trying to be, there are difficult decisions to make that can lead to surprises and less-than-friendly responses. That's why there are lawyers.

Another Five-Card Reading

Sometimes the best advice in a five-card reading does not come from the fourth and fifth cards but from elsewhere in the layout.

Lynn Nicholas is a massage therapist who also works with other modalities such as sound healing. She came to me seeking some general guidance concerning her career. The first card I drew was the King of Clubs, a card representing a stable, secure, and approachable man in her past. Lynn immediately recognized her father here. Then I drew the Jack of Spades. This card indicates a person who is unhappy with their current situation. It usually indicates a person other than the querent, but my intuition was telling me that the card was speaking of Lynn herself this time.

Then I drew the third card, the Jack of Hearts. This card represents someone you have known for a while and in whom you have some kind of emotional investment. In this reading, it was Lynn's fiancé.

Notice that all three cards representing Lynn's past, present, and future were court cards. Although she was asking about her career, this reading was clearly about people.

The fourth card I drew, revealing what was or would be driving Lynn forward, was the Six of Hearts, a card of arguments and emotional discord. It was her work environment that was pushing her to look at alternative opportunities. And what was holding her back? For that, I drew the Six of Diamonds. Financial issues were the problem here.

This reading is saying that there are conflicting forces in Lynn's life right now. Annoyances at work combined with financial concerns have her in an unhappy position. But this is a temporary condition. There are people in her life, particularly her father and her fiancé, who can lend her strength as she gets through this rough patch. And, of course, the future card in this reading is the card representing her fiancé, which suggests that he is the light at the end of her tunnel!

A Twelve-Card Reading

There are times when you may want a broader, more comprehensive view of destiny. Kat Owensby is an intelligent, attractive aspiring writer who was getting ready to move across the United States to continue her education. This was a perfect time to use the twelve-card layout.

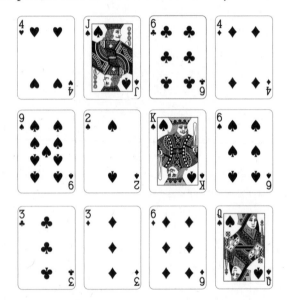

The card representing Kat herself is the Four of Hearts, describing her friendly and stable disposition. This is immediately followed by the Nine of Spades in the second position, representing her resources, what she has to work with. The Nine of Spades cautions us to be more responsible. Kat will need to manage her resources well and consider the consequences of each of her decisions as she moves into this new phase of her life.

The Three of Clubs in the third position suggests that there might be some problems ahead with people outside of Kat's immediate family whom she is nevertheless close to. This card indicates that Kat herself will be the cause of the conflict. But the cards always indicate what might happen. We have free will to change the future. The Three of Clubs is a warning for Kat to be careful in her interactions with the people close to her at this point in her life.

The fourth card represents someone or something from the past that has some influence on present and future events. Here I drew the Jack of Spades, a card representing a deceitful person. Kat immediately recognized this as an ex-boyfriend. As I said, the fourth card in this layout describes the past, but you will soon see how it affects other cards in the reading. In card divination, each card can be influenced by other cards that appear. You have to look at the entire pattern that the cards are making.

A wild card, the Two of Spades, is in the fifth position. This position in a twelve-card reading often references parties and social interactions, but in this reading it is speaking about Kat's creative drive. Her continuing education will focus on creative writing, and here we see that there will be some unexpected developments in that area of her life. These could be very positive developments, but

Kat should be prepared to find her creativity flowing in directions she has not yet envisioned.

In the sixth position, revealing duties and obligations, we see the Three of Diamonds. Clearly, at this point in her life, Kat should avoid committing herself to any long-term responsibilities.

The next two cards I drew are related to each other. In this layout, the seventh card represents your partner, often a romantic partner, although it could also represent a business partner or even a really close friend. And just as the second card represents your resources, the eighth card represents what your partner has to offer.

Kat does have a current boyfriend. The Six of Clubs in the seventh position indicates that he could soon become ill. Of more interest, however, is the King of Spades in the eighth position. This King can represent a man who is stable and reliable. It can also represent an enemy. My intuition told me that in this reading the card is not speaking of an enemy, but I could not help but sense a connection between the King of Spades and the Jack falling in Kat's fourth position. These cards told me that the relationship she had with the man in her past is shadowing the relationship that she now has with her current boyfriend. She needs to work at separating her feelings for these two men to ensure the health of her new relationship.

The card in the ninth position is stating the obvious. This is the position representing travel as well as experiences that expand the mind or the spirit. Here we have the Six of Diamonds, a card indicating a lack or loss of financial resources. It is no secret that college is expensive and that college students usually struggle with finances. Kat will have to budget carefully after she moves, but this will come as a surprise to absolutely nobody.

The tenth card is always a focal point since it represents the future. Every other card in this layout could speak of something that already exists, but the tenth card is something that has yet to manifest. For Kat, this is the Four of Diamonds. It is an extremely positive omen. The Four of Diamonds is stability. It can be financial stability, but it also speaks of a sound and stable reputation.

The eleventh position has to do with long-term relationships. Usually, but not always, these are relationships that already exist. Here we have the Six of Spades, which, like the previous Six of Diamonds, is simply reminding Kat of something that she already knows. The Six of Spades represents a depletion of energy. Just as Kat knows that she will be dealing with some financial hardship, it is no secret that her current long-term friendships will have a diminished role in her life. This is not necessarily a bad thing. The card may even be giving her a little advice, suggesting that she prepare herself to release old ties and open herself to future friendships and experiences.

Finally, we come to the twelfth position, which can reveal secrets or point out something that could hold you back. We see the Queen of Spades. This Queen can either represent a woman in your life or represent duty in some way or another. My intuition drew me to the latter interpretation. Here we have another example of how cards influence each other in a reading. Remember the Three of Diamonds in the sixth position? That card is counseling Kat to avoid committing to long-term responsibilities. Here, with the Queen of Spades, we see more of this. Kat has reached a transition point in her life. As she steps into the future, she needs to avoid making commitments, for now, that will tie her down and prevent her from attaining her ultimate goals.

Create Your Own Style!

The previous examples were all real readings given using the layouts presented in this book, but feel free to experiment with other layouts. Tarot readers often use a Celtic Cross layout using ten cards. I have also seen a variant of the simple past-present-future layout where three cards are drawn to reveal past influences, three describe the present situation, and three are for future possibilities. The three past cards are interpreted collectively to reveal influences leading to the current situation, then the three present cards are interpreted collectively, followed by the three future cards. In each set of three, the cards clarify and define each other.

You might want to lay out a past-present-future reading in a vertical formation rather than a horizontal one, with the present arising from the past and in turn supporting the future. Or, as I mentioned earlier, it may feel more natural to you to arrange the twelve cards in a twelve-card layout in a circle rather than a grid.

You may even feel drawn to create a completely unique layout for your own use, with your own concept for each card's position. There is nothing wrong with this. After all, every layout was created by somebody at some point in time. What matters is whether or not the pattern works. When creating a new layout, be objective and keep track of your results to ensure that your system is as effective as the proven layouts described here are.

As you work with the cards, you will probably come to favor one particular layout. Each layout has its own strengths and weaknesses. The important thing is to find one or more layouts that speak to you.

Nine

When and Where to Read Cards

A good reader will develop their own relationship with the cards. This is reflected not only in the decks that a reader uses and any unique, individual interpretations of the cards, but also in where and how often the reader consults the cards. These latter decisions define the reader as much as anything else. For some people, cartomancy is a private and personal activity. At the other end of the spectrum are people who will read cards at parties, at psychic fairs, or for anyone who asks. Likewise, one reader might practice the art only in a secluded, semiprivate space, while somebody else might be completely comfortable drawing cards on a city bus.

As we saw in the preceding chapter, different card layouts lend themselves to different kinds of readings. These layouts also affect how often you can effectively consult the cards. As a general rule, a smaller layout can be used more frequently than a complex one. This is in respect to an individual querent, of course. There is no reason why you cannot sit down and give twelve-card readings to five different people, because each person is only receiving one reading. On the other hand, if you draw twelve cards for yourself and repeat this four more times, it will devolve into a meaningless mess. You were given your answer and you ignored it. A cartomancer approaches the cards with respect. If they are treated like a parlor game, that is exactly what they will become.

A single card reading can be done every day. When you begin working with cards, it is a good idea to draw a single card for yourself each day, ideally in the morning. Do not immediately look up the meaning of the card. First ask yourself what, if anything, the card is saying to you. Think about both the suit and the numerological significance of the card, but trust your intuition as well. Only then should you look up the card's meaning, if you do not remember it. And do not be discouraged if you cannot remember what a card means. This is perfectly normal when you are starting out. It seemed to take me forever to master the suit of Clubs.

After you draw and interpret the card, keep it in mind throughout the rest of the day. How does it apply to the events unfolding around you? What do you think the card is trying to tell you? Unless you follow the exact same routine every day, you will notice that the cards change meanings to adapt to your activities and environment. What a card reveals depends, in part, on where you are, who you are, and what your immediate plans are. The King of Clubs represents a stable, mature man, but it is highly unlikely that you are going to meet this guy, or any other man, if you do not leave your home. In a situation where it is highly unlikely that you will be meeting anyone that day, the King of Clubs might instead be saying that you need to work on building more stability in your own life. This is where your intuition comes into play when interpreting cards.

Drawing a daily card will help you develop a relationship with your deck and understand your cards. Even when you have mastered the cards and know the meaning of each one by heart, a daily single card reading can help you maintain and hone your skill.

Whichever layout you use, one card per day is a good general guideline as to how often you should consult the cards. In other words, if you do a past-present-future reading, this should not be repeated for the same person (whether yourself or somebody else) until three days have passed. Likewise, twelve-card readings should be spaced at least twelve days apart.

Keep in mind that these are absolute minimums. Personally, I do not like to do a twelve-card reading more than once every two or three months. If you read too frequently for the same person, it all breaks down into a garbled mess. It becomes a game rather than a serious consultation.

This guideline is for *general* card readings for one person. If you have a specific question and draw three cards, there is of course no reason why you cannot draw three cards again later that same day for insight into an entirely different issue. Likewise, you could give a dozen five-card readings for a dozen different people in one evening if you are up to the task.

You do need to practice reading the cards to gain any real mastery of the art. Drawing a single card each morning is a good habit to establish, but it will not help you understand how the cards interact with each other. Returning to our example of the King of Clubs, this King's message might be clarified by its position in a three-card reading, as well as by the other two cards that you draw. Your intuition is still important, but with this layout you may also have a couple of clues to work with. It presents relationships between the cards.

The twelve-card layout presents an even more complex web of relationships. In the first position, as card 1, the King of Clubs represents you, even if you are a woman. If the same card is card 11, it is directing you to a stable and reliable friend. The meaning of the King of Clubs is then further defined by the other cards in the reading. In fact, until you have some experience with it, the twelve-card reading can be a little overwhelming, and there are nuances that you will undoubtedly miss. This is not something to worry about. Your intuition will direct your attention to the more important patterns. With practice, you will begin to see more relationships between the cards. This is why some people prefer to lay out the twelve cards in a circle, positioned like the numbers on a clock. The layout you choose should be the one that allows you to more readily notice how the cards influence each other.

But if you should do a complex reading like this only every two weeks or so, how can you gain experience with a twelve-card layout? The best way to get more practice is to give readings to other people. Until you have some skill in the art, it is best to limit this to a few close friends or family members who understand that you are still learning. By reading for other people, you will also see how the messages of the cards change according to the querent's needs, desires, and lifestyle. Our King of Clubs will likely mean something completely different for a fifty-year-old man than for a twenty-year-old woman. Age, gender, marital status, sexual orientation, and economic situation are all factors that can influence a card's interpretation.

Many municipalities have "fortune-telling" laws, but this should not be a concern if you are reading for friends and family members. Those laws were established to control charlatans who use cartomancy and other forms of divination as a cover to swindle naïve or desperate people. They will not apply to you, since you are not taking any money for your readings.

Eventually, after a few years' experience, you may feel that you are skilled enough to charge for your readings. If so, be sure to find out what laws apply to this in your locality. If you have the skill and talent, and if your readings are in high demand, it is not unreasonable to expect some compensation for your time and effort, assuming the law allows for this. As a rule, though, I do not recommend this, because as soon as you accept money for reading cards, you have created a conflict of interest. Your querents are now your customers, and on some level, conscious or not, you now have a motive to please these people, to "give them their money's worth." Some readers can sidestep this obstacle, but for others it can influence their work.

As a beginner, of course, you will not be charging money, and giving readings to other people is an excellent way to gain practice. But not everybody will have friends and family members who appreciate divination. Even if you do, you may not feel comfortable reading for other people. This is not uncommon, especially when you are just starting to learn how to read cards. But if you cannot or do not want to read for other people, how do you gain experience with the cards?

First, read for yourself on a regular basis. You are already doing this if you are doing a single card reading each morning. In addition to this, consider a past-present-future reading every week. Pick a specific day and time to do this reading, like Friday evenings or Sunday afternoons. Write down your interpretation of the three cards so you can refer back to it as the week unfolds. If you keep this in a journal, you can also record any personal interpretations you discover in your readings.

Every three months or so, lay out a twelve-card reading for yourself. When to do this more complex reading can be an arbitrary decision on your part, or it can be timed with something you find meaningful, like a solstice or an equinox.

If you want to get in more practice than this but do not have anyone you can comfortably do readings for, try doing those readings anyway *without the other person's presence*. If you do this, keep in mind that nothing you see in the cards can be shared with anyone, even with the person you drew the cards for, since you do not have that person's consent. These readings can help you learn how to interpret cards for different kinds of people. Even if you never ever intend to read cards for others, it will deepen your own understanding of the cards and the messages they reveal. Choose people of different ages and genders to get a feel for how the cards read for diverse querents.

Choosing a Location for Your Readings

We have looked at how often to consult the cards. Now let us consider where we want to do this.

If you read cards in your own home, you can have considerable control over the environment. When giving a reading at home, whether for yourself or for a friend or family member, it can help to set the stage before pulling out your cards. As with meditation or prayer, creating a conducive environment is another way to prepare yourself for a reading. The design of this environment is entirely up to you. There may be a chair, a library table, or some other furnishing in your house that feels especially empowering. At a minimum, you need to be able to sit comfortably at an open working surface. If it is possible for you to do this using a favorite chair or table, by all means do so. Over time, the very act of sitting down in this chosen workspace will signal your mind to focus on the act of divination.

Whether or not you have a special workspace for your readings, consider drawing, placing, and interpreting your cards by candlelight. Turn off all electric lighting in the room and use a single white or beeswax taper candle for illumination. This will direct your attention to the immediate area where you are laying out the cards, allowing outside distractions to more readily fade away from your awareness. For religious reasons, some readers like to use two or even three candles for this, but one is sufficient for illumination.

Some readers also find incense to be empowering. For a divinatory incense, mix together equal parts of dried garden sage (*Salvia officinalis*) and dried rosemary (*Rosmarinus officinalis*). For an extra boost, you can add a few drops of nutmeg oil to this, but it is not necessary. Burn the blended herbs over a charcoal block while you interpret the cards. This is more than you need to do if you are drawing only one or three cards, but it works quite nicely with a twelve-card reading. In addition to using this incense during a reading, I will sometimes burn these herbs and pass my cards individually through the smoke to attune them to the purpose of divination.

If you are reading for other people, you may often find yourself giving readings somewhere other than your own home. It may be a location where you are unable to use candles or incense as part of your process. That is perfectly fine. All of these things are aids, not necessities. And even if you read only for yourself, there will be times when you are away from home and you want to consult your cards. Creating an empowering environment for reading cards does not confine you to that location. You can give readings any time, anywhere, as long as you have a deck of cards—within reason. It should go without saying that you would not want to read cards outside during a thunderstorm!

Give Yourself a Break!

If you have an outgoing personality, even if you do not give readings for personal monetary gain, there may be occasions where you are a reader at a party or for a benefit. These are great opportunities to understand your cards as they relate to different people. It is especially important to be well grounded when going into an event like this. Remember to take breaks and give yourself time to center, and do not feel obligated to give anyone a reading if you feel uncomfortable with that person for any reason. If that happens, lay out the cards and then apologize and say that you are not getting any impressions. This extricates you from giving a reading without insulting your would-be querent. If you are at a benefit and they have paid for a reading, you obviously cannot take their money or ticket. There is an intimacy in looking at someone else's fortune. It is not something that you should ever feel compelled to do if your heart is telling you not to.

Even if you do a daily single card reading, there may be times when you have a specific question later in the day. Maybe you had an annoying day at work, just as the Four of Spades hinted at earlier that morning, and now a couple of friends want to know if you would like to go out to a club with them. Has the Four of Spades run its course, or will a night out prove to be as annoying as the rest of your day has been? Draw another card and find out! Think of it as a clarification card.

With enough practice, you will find that your cards come alive and speak to you in ways that transcend the finite interpretations presented in a book.

Ten

The Ethics of Divination

When interpreting cards for another person, the reader looks beyond the ordinary, exterior mask that the other person presents to the world. There is an intimate aspect to divination. For this reason, it is important to set boundaries for your own protection and that of the person you are reading for. Readers who ignore the ethics of divination are very likely to make enemies and develop bad reputations.

You should never read for anyone else without that person's consent. Bear in mind that reading *for* someone is not the same as reading *about* someone. You will be looking at other people even if you never give a reading for anyone but yourself. If the Five of Hearts and the Seven of Spades suggest a new romantic relationship in your future, somebody else is obviously going to be involved! In the twelve-card layout, at least a third of the cards almost always represent other people in your life.

In the previous chapter, intentionally drawing cards for people who are not present was suggested as a way of honing your skill. But the reader who does this is ethically bound not to share anything seen in the cards with others. The reading is solely for your own practice. In the same way, if you are reading for yourself and the cards indicate that your boyfriend is thinking about breaking up, you cannot tell him what you have seen. You can keep an eye on him and perhaps even have an indirect talk about where your relationship is going, but you cannot indicate that your suspicions came from a card reading.

Now, when I say "you cannot," I obviously mean you should not. You *can* tell your boyfriend whatever you want, but it is not going to go well if your accusations are based on a card reading. People who know anything about divination will understand that you might pick up something about them, but nobody wants to feel like you are spying on them. Furthermore, even if there is nothing unpleasant about what you see in the cards, not everyone wants to know what the future holds. Some people find it very uncomfortable, while others object for religious reasons.

Consider What You Say

Some years ago, I had the honor of facilitating a wedding for a young couple. It was a lovely summer wedding. Not long after the wedding, a distraught Tarot reader contacted the new bride and told her that her marriage was not going to last. It would end disastrously. As you might expect, the young woman was more than a little upset by this pronouncement. Of course, it was wrong for the Tarot reader to say this to her without first having her consent to give a reading, but that was just the tip of the ethics iceberg. I am sad to say that the marriage did not work out. It ended in betrayal and abuse by both parties. And to this day I have to wonder, *how much did that prediction contribute to the outcome?*

Even if you do have consent to do a reading, it is terribly important to consider everything you say. When you are reading for someone else, you are looking at where they are at that precise moment in time. Anything happening in that moment can influence your querent's future. There is a world of difference between saying "your marriage is doomed" and saying "you may be facing some marital challenges in the near future." The first example implies an unalterable future, a futile existence where there is no free will. The second example simply suggests possible future influences.

How do you think the new bride felt toward the Tarot reader who told her that her marriage was going to come to a disastrous end? Before this occurred, the two women had been friends. Afterward, the young woman never felt the same way again about the Tarot reader. The reader damaged her own reputation and ruined their friendship.

Words Have Power

Words have power. It is your responsibility, when giving a reading, to avoid manipulating the querent in any way. Every one of us has a personal agenda; there are things and events that please us and things that we do not care for. Here, the ancient Delphic teaching to "know thyself" is crucial for every reader. The ethical reader is mindful of their own agenda and takes care not to let this influence the reading. Your goal as a reader is to help your querents; it is not your place to manipulate them.

I once listened as a reader interpreted cards for someone whom he was obviously physically attracted to. According to this reader, the two of them had been lovers in a former life. It was easy to see what was happening. The reader was interested in kindling a romance and was insinuating that a romantic relationship had already existed. I do believe in reincarnation, but a story like this should immediately raise a red flag. And that is exactly how the querent reacted. The reader accomplished nothing except to tarnish his own reputation. Even if the ploy had worked, it would have been an extreme breach of ethics.

Regardless of your intentions, you should avoid shaping the querent's future to the best of your ability. This obviously is not an issue when reading cards for yourself, but good, conscientious readers are always mindful that their words can influence a querent's decisions and actions.

The Margin of Error

Because of the inevitable margin of error inherent in divination, it is important not to make absolute assertions when giving a reading. I do not care how talented you are, sometimes your predictions will be completely wrong. Maybe you interpreted the cards incorrectly. For one reason or another, sometimes the things you see in the cards just do not happen the way you predicted. The primary reason why you should never make absolute statements suggesting an unalterable destiny is because that is not how the universe works. Maybe the querent will change their behaviors and actions after the reading, leading to a different outcome. The future is constantly unfolding from the present, shaped by our actions and decisions. You can never know for certain what will happen in the future. In all forms of divination, what you are seeing are probabilities, not definite, absolute results.

The margin of error is actually a very good thing. If you do see something like challenges to your querent's marriage, the querent can take steps to successfully overcome those challenges. A failed relationship is not a foregone conclusion. If we had no influence over our own destiny, there would be no point in divination at all. It would be pure voyeurism.

Speaking in absolutes, as if destiny cannot be changed, can actually sabotage your querent no matter what the cards seem to be saying. We have already seen how the young bride's marriage may have been sabotaged in part by the Tarot reader. Her marriage might have failed anyway, but being told that it was going to fail certainly did not help. But what if a similar thing had taken place with a more fortunate prediction? Imagine that the reader had told this same woman that she would be receiving a big career promotion. The woman might have taken for granted that this would happen and not put in the effort required to actually take her career in the direction she desired. There is a world of difference between saying "you are going to get a promotion" and saying "I see some very positive influences concerning your career."

An ethical reader always ensures that querents understand they have control over their own destiny.

Of course, if you read for other people, there will be times when you see what looks like a crisis. I do not know what the Tarot reader saw that foretold of a failed marriage, but I can imagine an equally disastrous reading with playing cards. As an example, let us assume that my querent is a married woman and that I am doing a twelve-card reading. The Four of Clubs comes up in the second position, the Six of Spades in the seventh position, and the Queen of Diamonds in the eighth. The second position indicates the querent's strengths and assets, and the Four of Clubs in this position tells us that she is oblivious to what is happening around her. The seventh position represents her spouse, so the Six of Spades tells me that there is a depletion of energy in their relationship. Next to this, in the eighth position, we see the Queen of Diamonds, a woman with an agenda, and her position in the reading indicates that this other woman has a significant place right now in the husband's life.

Superficially, it looks like the husband is seeing another woman who fulfills whatever it is that he is missing in his marriage. I am not going to say this to my querent, though, at least not in those words. First, there is the inevitable margin of error. Maybe I have interpreted the cards wrong. Second, expressing a prediction in this way could become a self-fulfilling prophecy, leading the querent to take actions that ultimately destroy a salvageable marriage. And third, however dire the reading might seem, my querent has the right to shape her own destiny, or to at least make the attempt. The future is never set in stone until it flows into the past.

Instead, I would suggest that the querent be mindful of her marriage and perhaps talk with her husband about how to spice things up a little. I would probably go so far as to say that I see "a woman" in her husband's life, and that this woman should be herself. Do you see how this empowers my querent in a way that an absolute prediction does not? Expressing what is seen in the cards as influences rather than destiny allows that person to have some control over the situation.

It is equally important that you not lie to the querent and pretend that all is well when the cards are clearly saying something else. If you are reading cards for somebody, that person has put their trust in you. It is unethical to betray that trust, even if you are doing it to spare the querent's feelings. By following the above guidelines, your querents will still be empowered to take charge of their future, even when your readings are not all rainbows and butterflies.

I said that your querent will put their trust in you, but this is not always the case. Occasionally you will be approached by a skeptic who either views divination as a joke or intends to disprove your ability. You are under no obligation to read for people like this. If you choose to do so, however, you should follow the same ethical guidelines that you would when reading cards for a legitimate querent.

There are other reasons that you may not want to read cards for someone. The other person may simply give you an uncomfortable feeling, even if it is nothing that you can identify. Or you may lay out the cards and see a truly dreadful result that you do not want to share with the querent for some reason. Again, you are never obligated to read cards. I have told people that the cards are not revealing anything to me. And more often than not when I do this, it really is true: the cards just seem to be a confused mess when I look down at them. But whether or not it is true is unimportant. I am not giving the potential querent false information about their future; I am simply not sharing information at all. Of course, you cannot take money from someone for a reading and then not give them one, even if the money is for a charity benefit. In a situation like this, you must return any gratuity when you decline to give the reading.

Finally, it should go without saying that you should never ever offer to help the querent change the future in any way. As a card reader, you are an observer. In the next chapter, we will look at using playing cards for working magic, but this is something I advise doing only for yourself or for someone you are very close to, like a family member. I would not recommend offering that service to your querents. Anti-divination ordinances were originally enacted because of criminals posing as readers who then "helped" their clients avoid some unfortunate fate. The help almost inevitably had the collateral effect of relieving the client of a substantial sum of cash. By offering to cast spells for anyone other than close friends and family, you could be perceived as someone connected with that kind of activity, even if that was not at all your intention.

Eleven

Spellcasting with Playing Cards

There are readers who are satisfied with simply seeing what the future may hold for them. Witches are more interested in shaping their future.

Anyone who can read playing cards is capable of working a spell with those cards. This is not something unique to playing cards; the same is true with a Tarot deck. As when reading cards, there are ethical issues involved when casting a spell for another person. This is something you should do only for yourself or your loved ones. Even then you should have their consent. Not everyone wants to have a spell cast on them, even if the intention is entirely benevolent.

The basic principle behind casting a spell with cards is really quite simple. When giving a reading, you draw cards at random and lay them out. When casting a spell, you intentionally choose the cards that you want to see in your future and place them in a layout with equal intention. Instead of asking what the future holds, you lay it out purposefully. Of course, the magic that powers this comes from within you. It is a talent. And like any other talent, there are people who are more gifted at this than others, but almost all of us have at least some ability to weave a little magic into our lives.

A card spell requires seven days to complete, so you will need a place where you can leave some cards and a candle undisturbed for a full week. Ideally this will also be a place where you will have some privacy while working the spell. If you are a witch, you probably already have a specially prepared altar or similar working space for this. Otherwise, a desk or table or similar level surface will serve the same purpose.

The second thing to do is to decide how you will lay out the cards for your spell. For some spells, the three-card layout will suffice. The central card is chosen to express your basic desire, and the two other cards are then placed to either side of this one to further clarify your intention. But for a broader, life-changing spell, the twelve-card layout often works better. The twelve-card layout can create sweeping changes in your life, though, so it should be used only if that is what you are trying to achieve.

When choosing cards for your spell, do not forget the Deuces. All four of these are wild cards. The purpose of your spell is usually to create change in some way, and the Deuces can serve as "batteries" to get things moving. In a three-card layout, you would not use these for your central card, but you might throw in a Deuce as one of the other two cards. In a twelve-card layout, you could put a Deuce in any position where you do not have a specific intention in mind. The choice of which Deuce to use may depend on what you are trying to achieve with your spell. The Two of Hearts is best for spells concerning romance or friendship, whereas the Two of Spades is a better choice if you want to get a new project off the ground. If you are trying to get that raise, use the Two of Diamonds. The Two of Clubs is your best choice for a spell to nurture personal, internal changes.

In addition to the cards that you have chosen, you will need a candle for your spell. A blue candle can be used for any card spell, but you may want to choose a different color to better reflect your intention:

Color	Intention
Red	Healing, lust, romance
Orange	Courage, resolve
Yellow	Friendship, knowledge, intellect
Green	Prosperity, fertility
Blue	Protection, can be used for any spell
Purple	Power, influence

Place the candle on the altar or working surface and then lay out your cards in front of it. As you place each card, think about what that card represents and how it will manifest in your life.

If you are working a spell on behalf of a loved one, you will also need a link to connect your magic with that person. This link could be a photograph of the loved one, some of their hair or nail clippings, or anything that the person has had intimate contact with. A piece of jewelry works well for this purpose. This link should be placed between the candle and the cards.

After you have everything in place, surround the cards and candle with a circle of salt. This will focus your power as you work your spell over the coming week. It does not need to be a huge pile of salt, but it should form a complete circle around both the cards and the candle as well as your link, if you are using one. You are now ready to begin the spell.

The best time to begin your card spell is between sunset on Tuesday night and sunset on Wednesday. This period of time is ruled by the planet Mercury, which governs communication and magic. If Wednesday is inconvenient, though, you can start the spell at any time during the week. The important thing is to work the spell at the same time on each of the seven days.

When you are ready to begin, safely light the candle. If you wish, you may also light some incense as an offering to an appropriate deity, but this is optional. After lighting the candle, sit with your cards for seven minutes. Envision the outcome of your spell. See it manifested in your life not as something that is going to happen but as if it has already come to pass. Let the cards that you chose for your spell be a part of this meditation. Focus your gaze on each card and remember why you chose it. Remember what it represents as you visualize your manifested desire.

After seven minutes, extinguish the candle and say "So mote it be" or "Amen" or whatever verbal statement gives you a sense of closure. It is fine if your visualization runs longer than seven minutes, but it should never be less than this.

Repeat the process the following day at the same time. Light the candle. Light incense if you wish. Then sit with your cards for seven minutes. This must be done seven times, once each day for seven days. Remember, seven is the number of completion.

Enhancing Your Spell

If you find yourself drawn to magic, you can enhance this spell in several ways.

If you are a practitioner of ceremonial magic or a follower of Wicca, you may want to cast a magic circle around your working space before beginning the spell. Unlike the circle of salt surrounding your cards, this larger ritual circle does not need to remain in place after you have done your daily work. It should be dismantled as you would do after any other ritual and then recast the following day.

Or you may follow a spiritual or magical path with an entirely different means of creating sacred space. Any prayers or rituals that help you focus on the work at hand are appropriate when working magic with playing cards.

Another way to enhance your spell is by beginning it on a day ruled by a planet that governs or rules what you hope to achieve. I suggest Wednesday as a good day to begin the spell because it is ruled by Mercury, a planet that governs magic. Keep in mind, though, that the natural "day" starts at sunset the night before. We still have vestiges of this in modern culture with our celebrations of Christmas Eve, New Year's Eve, and even All Hallows' Eve (Hallowe'en). In the same way, Tuesday night can also be thought of as "Wednesday Eve." In fact, in Old English it was called Woden's Night (*Wodnesniht*), which preceded Woden's Day, or what we now call Wednesday.

Wednesday is usually a good day for casting any playing card spell, but you can give your magic a little boost by beginning your spell on a day conducive to your goal. Each day of the week is governed by one of the seven visible planets as follows:

Day	Planet	Governs
Sunday	Sun	Growth, knowledge, health, mental strength
Monday	Moon	Protection, secrets, psychic ability
Tuesday	Mars	Courage, health, physical strength, victory
Wednesday	Mercury	Magic, communication, commerce
Thursday	Jupiter	Prosperity, success, growth, health
Friday	Venus	Love, lust, emotions, beauty
Saturday	Saturn	Stability, security, binding

Moon Phases

The phase of the moon can also affect your spell. To bring something into your life or to empower something, begin your spell between the night on which you see that the first crescent of the new moon has appeared in the sky and the night when it becomes a half-moon. This way, your entire spell will be worked while the moon is *waxing*, or growing larger. You want to work the entire spell, which takes seven days, during the waxing moon. If you begin the spell after the moon is half full, then the moon will be waning when you finish, which is contrary to your purpose.

Conversely, if you want to bring an end to something, to banish something from your life or at least diminish its influence, then begin your spell after the full moon but before it has diminished to less than a half-moon. Again, this is to ensure that the entire spell is worked while the moon is *waning*, or diminishing in size.

The important consideration is whether the moon is waxing or waning. Ideally, if you are confident that you can time your spell correctly, then the best time to begin a spell is the night of the half-moon, which will allow you to finish the spell at the full moon (for a spell to bring something into your life) or at the dark of the moon (for a banishing spell). Unfortunately, this will not always fall on an auspicious day of the week. But that is a key difference between an adept and a novice: the former has the ability to determine the best time to begin a spell, given the variables. It can sometimes be difficult to choose the best day when you are first starting out, but over time it gets easier. Here is where your intuition becomes important again. Trust your instincts.

Herbs

A circle of salt is a reliable way to focus the energy of your card spell, but this can be enhanced by substituting specific herbs for the salt. I use plants a lot in my own magic, so surrounding the cards and the candle (if I am using one) with appropriate herbs is something that works very well for me. As with the salt, you do not need a large pile of plant material, but the herbs should completely enclose the cards (and candle) that you have set out.

The herbs you use should be appropriate for your goal. It is usually easier to work with dried herbs, but this is certainly not essential. Choose one or more herbs that reflect what you are hoping to achieve. Here are some ideas:

Purpose	Herbs
To increase courage	Mullein, black tea, thyme, yarrow
General happiness	Hyacinth blossoms, lavender, St. John's wort
Magical healing	Lemon balm, bay leaves, mint, cinnamon, thyme
For love	Basil, cloves, dill, rose petals, rosemary
General luck	Daffodils, holly, violets
Lust	Cinnamon, daisies, dill, parsley, southernwood

Purpose	Herbs
Mental strength	Lily of the valley, rosemary, rue
To promote harmony	Gardenia blossoms, lavender, pennyroyal, violets
Protection	Basil, bay leaves, dill, garlic
Success	Lemon balm, cinnamon, clover

You can surround your cards with a blend of both salt and herbs if you wish. I usually use one or the other, but there are times when a combination of these may be your best choice, especially for spells for protection or health.

Galdor

Finally, you can empower your spell with your own words. This technique was known to the early English people as *galdor*. The use of speech was an essential part of magic. Even today, in the English language we refer to a magical working as a *spell*, a word that evolved from *spellian*, an Old English verb meaning to speak or proclaim. Galdor is the art of working magic through speech. Indeed, language itself is a magical art, with the power to help or to harm. This power can take your playing card spell to a higher level.

The magic of language is widely accepted and can be found in popular culture, such as when people speak personal affirmations. But these practices often overlook how the words themselves—the sounds they make, the patterns of their consonants and vowels—have an innate power. Stating your intention as you light your spell candle can be effective, but you will be rewarded with greater success by choosing the right words to empower that statement.

In Old English charms, words were often empowered through the use of alliteration. This is using the same consonant sound at the beginning of each word, as in "Peter Piper picked a peck of pickled peppers."

As an example, imagine that someone close to you was in an accident and you wanted to cast a spell with playing cards to help them recover quickly. You might do this with a three-card layout, choosing the Four of Diamonds (for stability) as your central card, and placing to either side of this the Nine of Hearts (for protection) and the Seven of Spades (indicating the situation or condition is improving). You might choose a red candle for healing and surround the candle and cards with a circle of dried lemon balm and bay leaves. With this arrangement, when you light the candle each time, you could say, "(Name of person)'s injuries are healing every day." You have stated your intention.

That is a nice affirmation, and it certainly will not hurt the success of the spell, but alliteration could produce a more powerful statement, such as "By balm and bay, I beckon a boon, bind blood to blood and bone to bone." This has energy behind it. This can stir the subconscious and awaken the magic within you.

Crafting a statement with alliteration requires more work than does our first simple affirmation. But if you are not willing to put in the work, why are you bothering with a spell at all?

Another way of empowering your words is through the use of rhyme. Rhymes tend to cling to us in a way that ordinary prose does not. This is why rhyming is often used in slogans, because it ensures that the message stays with us.

For our healing spell that we have been using as an example, a rhymed statement could be something like this: "By lemon balm and sweet bay leaf, let (name of person) know relief." Or, if you have surrounded your cards with salt instead of herbs, you could say, "Mind and body, spirit and soul, (name of person) shall now be whole." The exact words you use do not matter as long as they project the message of healing. The message is then given a boost by expressing it with rhyme or alliteration, or a combination of both.

The examples that I have given here use only one couplet. There is no reason that you cannot extend this into something longer. Spells often use a pair of couplets, with an incantation of four lines. If you use card spells frequently, you might go so far as to devise a second, all-purpose couplet that can be attached to any incantation. One example is "By all the power of land and sea, as my words proclaim, so let it be." This could be added to either of the healing couplets that I have presented here.

However you word your spell—however many lines you use and whether they rhyme or use alliteration, or both or neither—is a personal choice. If it works for you, then you are doing it right. And if you are doing it right, your fortune will indeed be in your hands.

Sample Spells

For the novice, crafting a spell can be challenging, so here are a few to get you started. You do not need to limit yourself to these, however. They are merely examples. Do not be afraid to design spells to address your own needs. Use the power of the cards to improve your life.

A Protection Spell

If you think someone is trying to hex you, this spell will protect you. The truth is that very few people purposefully cast curse spells, but people throw around minor curses all the time with their words and thoughts. If you have been having a run of bad luck, give this spell a try.

Begin your protection spell between sunset on Saturday and sunset on Sunday. This period of time is ruled by the Sun, the most protective of the planetary bodies.

Light a blue candle. If you'd like, you might also light some incense as an offering to a deity who offers protection or with whom you feel a particular connection.

For this spell, you will use the Four of Diamonds, the Nine of Hearts, and the Ace of Spades. Place the Nine of Hearts in front of the candle and then place the Four of Diamonds and the Ace of Spades to either side of this card. The Nine of Hearts is the central card because we want the spell to focus on protection. To one side of this is the Four of Diamonds, for stability. To the other side, the Ace of Spades represents triumph over obstacles. In this case, it is triumph over adverse influences. The placement of the cards is identical to that of a three-card reading, with the Four and the Ace acting as clarification cards to bolster your Nine of Hearts. Your statement is an intention of protection supported by your own stability and your ability to triumph over any harmful influences.

As you place the cards in front of the candle, meditate on what each one contributes to your spell: protection, stability, triumph. Focusing your thoughts on the meaning of each card is essential to the spell. You cannot just throw some cards down on a table and expect something to happen. The power comes from within you; the cards are merely tools to evoke that power.

Now surround the candle and cards with a circle of salt. Enhance this with galdor, using words to focus your power. If you are working the spell during the waxing (growing) moon, concentrate on building your innate defensive energy. If you are working during the waning (decreasing) moon, concentrate instead on your challenges or obstacles diminishing. As you surround the three cards with salt, say, "Circle of safety, salt of the sea, cast out all harm. So let it be!" The alliteration of the *s* sound is the sound made by the Sigil rune. In the Old English Rune Poem, Sigil is the sun and is a rune of guidance and protection.

A Love Spell

The best time to cast this love spell is between sunset on Thursday and sunset on Friday. This period of time is ruled by Venus, a planet associated with love. However, no matter which day you choose to begin, the spell should always be cast during the waxing moon.

The purpose of this spell is to bring romance into your life. It is a spell that you cast on yourself rather than on some other person. Yes, there are spells to make one specific person fall in love with you, but those are not love spells. They are really more like curses, with the intention of forcing another person to conform to your will. Even if we ignore the grossly unethical aspect of such a spell, spells like that are rarely successful. With this spell, instead of trying to bend someone to your desires, you are bringing romance into your life. This is why the spell is cast when the moon is waxing. It nurtures love.

Use a red candle for this love spell. If you want to offer incense to a deity, the Roman goddess Venus is an obvious choice, assuming you have some relationship with Venus. Praying for help from a deity to whom you have never before prayed or given offerings is akin to walking up to a random stranger and asking for some money. Yes, you might get what you ask for, but a friend is more likely to help you out. If you revere the gods of Kemet (Egypt), then either Hathor or Bastet would be good deities to offer a prayer to. A Welsh Pagan might pray to Branwen, while a Norse Pagan is likely to choose Frigg. The important thing is that you have some relationship with the deity.

Of course, the incense is entirely optional. When I was taught to perform this spell, it was presented as purely secular magic, with no prayers or offerings of any kind. If the incense offering is in any way confusing or awkward for you, then omit it.

Since this is a love spell, it should come as no surprise that we will be using the suit of Hearts, specifically the Five, Ten, and Seven of Hearts. These will be placed in a modified from-through-to format. The difference here is that all three cards will be representing future developments.

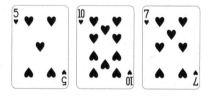

Light the candle as well as the incense, if you are including incense in your spell. Then lay out in front of the candle, from left to right, the Five of Hearts, the Ten of Hearts, and the Seven of Hearts. As you place each card, meditate on what it means in the magical statement you are sending out to the universe. The Five of Hearts represents social interactions, flirtations, parties. This card is reminding you that you do have to actually go out and meet other people if you hope to bring love into your life. On a magical level, this card draws you to social events where you can begin to meet people. Note that I said "people," not "your future love." This card represents the beginning, not the end goal.

The second card, the Ten of Hearts, is not the end goal either. The Ten of Hearts represents joy and extreme happiness. Here it speaks of that surge of joy that one feels when falling in love. But falling in love is not the same as true love. That is not what you are trying to achieve here. Or maybe it is. Some people love falling in love for the sake of the high that it brings. Here I am assuming you want something deeper and more permanent.

Finally, place the Seven of Hearts to the other side of the Ten. This is the card of complete emotional fulfillment, the marriage card.

Surround the candle and cards with a circle of red rose petals and say, "Wreathed around with roses red, I summon now the love I'll wed."

After completing this spell, make a point of going out and interacting with people. Join a club to meet people with common interests. Let people know that you are open to a romantic relationship. A spell can help draw the right person to you, but you do have to put yourself out in the world.

A Healing Spell

Healing is a general concept, so this spell has some variables depending on the nature of the affliction. Sunday, Tuesday, and Thursday are all good days for healing. Sunday is always auspicious, as it is ruled by the Sun. If you are attempting to restore or gain strength, however, Tuesday might be a better choice since it is governed by Mars. And by Tuesday, of course, I mean any time between sunset on Monday and sunset on Tuesday.

If your goal is to nurture growth, then Thursday, ruled by Jupiter, is the best day to begin your spell. Growth includes the healing of wounds, burns, and broken bones.

Likewise, the phase of the moon should also be taken into consideration when working this spell. Cast your magic when the moon is waxing if you want to nurture growth and healing. But if your intention is to stave off illness or reduce fever, do this spell during the waning moon. When it comes to healing, we usually do not have the luxury of waiting for the proper phase of the moon. There is usually some urgency involved, but card spells, which take a full week to complete, are intended for chronic, ongoing conditions. Think of this spell as magical extended care rather than magical first aid.

It should go without saying that any serious illness or injury should be seen to by a physician. Candles and cards can only do so much.

Light a red candle. Red is the color of blood. In northern European traditions, red is considered a magical color because blood is the essence of all animal life. In rune magic, runic inscriptions are painted red, often using blood, to evoke this power.

As with any card spell, you may also wish to offer incense to a deity of your choice at this time. A little cinnamon sprinkled on a charcoal block is a good choice for this spell, as cinnamon has magical healing properties.

Like the protection spell earlier in this chapter, this healing spell uses three cards to make a single, nonlinear statement.

Place the Four of Diamonds in front of the candle. This is your primary card to focus on. The Four of Diamonds represents stability and fortune. With respect to the body, it signifies good health. Envision the person you are casting the spell for as being whole and happy.

Holding this image in your mind, place the Two of Hearts to one side of the Four of Diamonds, then place the Two of Spades to the other side. Remember that the Deuces signify both balance and change. As wild cards, they also emphasize whatever card they fall next to, in this case the Four of Diamonds.

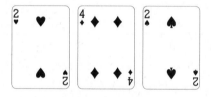

Surround the candle and cards with either a circle of salt or a circle of healing herbs (such as mint or thyme) while saying, "Mind and body, spirit and soul, (name of person) shall now be whole."

Twelve-Card Spells

The examples given so far have been relatively simple three-card spells intended for specific purposes. The twelve-card spell is a more complex working that creates sweeping changes throughout your life. It is identical to a twelve-card reading, but you are intentionally choosing the cards to place rather than drawing them by chance.

This is not a spell to be undertaken lightly. It could change your life in ways you did not anticipate, so be sure you are ready to go on that ride!

Due to the nature of this spell, I cannot tell you which cards to use. These must necessarily be your own choice. To give you an idea of how to choose your cards, let us use a hypothetical person whom we will call Lindsey. She is a young adult, recently married, and has just moved across the country, where she is pursuing a new career as a veterinary assistant. Since she does not know anyone in her new location yet, Lindsey decides to cast this twelve-card spell.

She places the Seven of Hearts in the first position, representing herself and how she is presented to the world. She is married and happy, and she wants people to see this. In the second position, representing her assets, she places the Eight of Diamonds for positive, steady growth.

In the third position, representing long-term relationships, Lindsey places the Four of Hearts to bring friends into her life. Perhaps she will even find a coven or grove that will accept her into their spiritual family.

She places the Ace of Clubs in the fourth position, her past, to acknowledge the events and experiences that have brought her to where she is now. She knows that the past and the future are connected, and she wants her strong, healthy past to influence what is yet to unfold in her life.

The Five of Diamonds goes in the fifth position. Lindsey does not have any creative hobbies, but she would like to have some fun, exciting social connections in her life.

For the sixth position, representing her duties and responsibilities, Lindsey chooses the Four of Diamonds. This will ensure stability and success in her new job as a veterinary assistant.

The seventh position, of course, represents her husband, Joshua. She does not want to change a single thing about him (although it would be nice if he would stop leaving his socks around the house). Joshua is an affable man, so Lindsey places the King of Hearts in this position to represent him. She then places the Nine of Hearts in the eighth position to extend its protection to him.

In the ninth position, Lindsey places the Two of Hearts. She does not anticipate any extensive physical traveling, but this position can also represent a spiritual journey. She is ready for something like that. This Deuce will shake things up a bit and should bring about a pleasant result.

For her tenth card, her future, she chooses the Ten of Diamonds. She is going for the gold. Lindsey wants to surround herself with friends. She wants to be popular. This card could have gone into the eleventh position, which specifically represents friends and social acquaintances, but Lindsey has reserved that spot for something else. She especially misses her best friend and would like to find someone to step into that place in her heart, so in the eleventh position she places the Queen of Clubs.

The twelfth position indicates secrets and deception, so you always want to be careful what you put there. Lindsey chooses the Two of Spades. It is one of the wild Deuces, and this one hints at a victory. She is allowing her subconscious its freedom while at the same time leading it to a positive effect.

The candle you use for this spell depends on the overall theme you want to pursue. A blue candle is always appropriate, but Lindsey will use a yellow candle because she wants to focus on making new friends. For your own spell, you will need to choose an appropriate candle color, day of the week, and phase of the moon. When I use this spell, I often like to arrange the twelve cards in a circle around the candle rather than as a grid (as shown here).

As you can see, a spell using twelve cards is quite complex. It is especially important to meditate on the meaning of each card as you place it in its respective position. Even so, it can be difficult to hold the concepts of all twelve cards in your mind. I recommend that you become proficient with the simpler three-card spells before trying this one.

Closure: After the Casting

After you have finished a spell, gather up the cards and return them to your deck. I thank the cards in order to release them from their task as I return them to the deck, and this is usually sufficient. By removing the cards from their positions in the layout, you are dismantling the statement that you made with your spell.

If you feel that your spell has left some lingering influence on your cards, you may of course cleanse them as described in chapter 1.

The salt used in your spell to encircle the cards and candle should be disposed of respectfully. Because of its solid yet soluble nature, the salt can be returned to either earth or water. If you bury the salt, you might say, "May you return to the earth." Alternatively, the salt can be washed down the drain of a sink as you say, "May you return to the sea." (This is a symbolic gesture. Unless you live near a coast, it is unlikely that the salt will literally enter the ocean.)

If, instead, you surrounded your cards with a circle of herbs, these can be burned as an offering to a deity of your choice. Even if you used fresh herbs, they should be dry and suitable for burning by the time you conclude your spell. If you included a prayer to a god or goddess while working the spell, that deity should obviously be the recipient of this offering. Otherwise, you may offer the herbs to any deity you have a relationship with. The deity does not necessarily have to be associated with the intention of your spell, although this is also something that might influence your decision.

Finally, to make sure that the spell can do its work, be sure to take action in the real world that can open a path to your desired outcome. This was mentioned in the description of the sample love spell earlier in this chapter. If you want to meet Mr. (or Ms.) Right, you cannot sit at home alone every night. Likewise, your healing spell will work much faster if the recipient can rest and recuperate. This is just common sense, but it is something that people often ignore. Magic influences possibilities; it does not shatter reality. Take whatever steps will help your card spell manifest in your life.

Then trust in your magic.

Conclusion

We have looked at the elemental and numerological correspondences in card divination, but I must emphasize again that the magic is within *you*, not in a deck of cards. Your cards are a tool to help unleash your own intuition.

To develop skill with a tool, you have to use it. Refer to this book when you need to, but let the cards speak to you through practice. Trust your feelings. Some cards may take on their own meaning for you, and that is okay. It is your intuition at work. The suit of Hearts corresponds to the element of Water and usually addresses emotional issues, but you may find, as you work with your own deck, that one card in the suit of Hearts predicts a change in your physical health. This does not mean that your own interpretation is wrong; it is merely personal and unique.

Every seer brings their own magic to the table when working with cards. The elemental and numerological correspondences presented in this book are intended to be guidelines, not absolute, rigid boundaries.

When working with your cards, put this book down. If you draw a card, do not automatically look up its interpretation. Instead, if nothing comes to you immediately, consider the card's number and its elemental correspondence. What does the card mean to you? After you have done this, look up the card and see how your own interpretation compares with the one in this book. If you continually look up the meaning of every card you draw, it will take much longer to master this skill. Looking up an interpretation can also obstruct your intuition, and you do not want to do that.

As you continue to practice, you will need to refer to the book less frequently. In time, the cards will come alive for you. The court cards may begin to remind you of specific people in your life. For me, the Queen of Hearts describes a Pagan priestess by the name of Alene who passed on from our world some years ago. She was one of the most kind and loving women I have ever known. Alene's love flowed through her in the role of mother, wife, lover, priestess, sister. This does not mean that the Queen of Hearts refers to Alene when it appears in my readings, although it certainly could. If you see in a court card someone you know, it is much easier to be mindful of the qualities that the card conveys.

The pip cards will also begin to come alive, evoking memories of specific events in your own life. When the Four of Hearts appears in a reading, I see myself as a teenager riding bikes with my friend Sue. That is not what the card means in the reading, of course, but it is how I connect with it. Sue lived across the street from me. We went through elementary and high school together and then went to the same college. We lost touch with each other for a while, but thanks to the internet, we have since reconnected. Although many years have gone by since we last saw each other, Sue represents emotional stability for me.

Memories and feelings like this will strengthen your intuitive connection with the cards, but it takes practice. The more readings you give for yourself and others, the more familiar you will become with the cards and the messages they can convey.

Likewise, if you work magic with your cards, you will become more comfortable with the cards with each spell you cast. This is because you have to consider the meaning of every card that you use in your spells. As with divination, the more you work magic with your deck of cards, the better you will get at it.

How long will it take you to master your cards? Well, I have been doing this for more than fifty years, and I am still learning new things, still seeing new meanings in the patterns that I lay out. Just as card readings for other people vary according to the person's age, gender, and interests, readings for yourself will slowly change over the years as your own life matures and changes.

So take up your deck, shuffle the cards, and see what fate has in store for you. This could be your first step on a wonderful journey exploring playing card divination and magic.

Keywords

This table is intended to provide a simple reminder in one or two words for the interpretation of each playing card. It also shows the elemental and numerological traits that influence these interpretations. As you work with your cards, you will develop your own relationship with them and may have personal interpretations that vary greatly from what is shown here.

	HEARTS (Emotion)	DIAMONDS (Fortune)	CLUBS (Transformation)	SPADES (Movement)
Ace: (Power)	Love	Good luck	Actualization	Triumph
Two: (Contrast)	Pleasant surprise	Unexpected event	Emotional change	Small victory
Three: (Seedlings)	Hobbies	"Not yet"	You are the problem	Hard work
Four: (Stability)	Friendship	Expected success	Reassess	Annoyances
Five: (Dynamic)	Parties, flirtations	Destiny	Lost cause	Obstacles
Six: (Depletion)	Harsh emotions	Loss of money	Conflict, frustration	No energy

To Write to the Author

If you wish to contact the author or would like more information about this book, please write to the author in care of Llewellyn Worldwide Ltd. and we will forward your request. Both the author and the publisher appreciate hearing from you and learning of your enjoyment of this book and how it has helped you. Llewellyn Worldwide Ltd. cannot guarantee that every letter written to the author can be answered, but all will be forwarded. Please write to:

Alaric Albertsson
℅ Llewellyn Worldwide
2143 Wooddale Drive
Woodbury, MN 55125-2989

Please enclose a self-addressed stamped envelope for reply, or $1.00 to cover costs. If outside the U.S.A., enclose an international postal reply coupon.

Many of Llewellyn's authors have websites with additional information and resources. For more information, please visit our website at http://www.llewellyn.com.

Seven: (*Completion*)	Marriage	Gain for another	Arguments	Improvements
Eight: (*Manifestation*)	A gift	Steady growth	Big changes	Caution
Nine: (*Wisdom*)	General protection	Protected money	Evolution	Responsibility
Ten: (*Force*)	Intense joy	Surge of fortune	Cold success	Sorrow
Jack: (*Younger person*)	Old Acquaintance	Ambitious person	Aggressive person	Deceitful
Queen: (*Mature female*)	Passion	Secret agenda	Maternal	Duty
King: (*Mature male*)	Easygoing	Secret agenda	Knowledgeable	An enemy